Depression in
Schizophrenia

PROGRESS IN PSYCHIATRY

Series

David Spiegel, M.D.
Series Editor

Depression in Schizophrenia

Edited by
Lynn E. DeLisi, M.D.

American Psychiatric Press, Inc.

1400 K Street, N.W.
Washington, DC 20005

Note: The authors have worked to ensure that all information in this book concerning drug dosages, schedules, and routes of administration is accurate as of the time of publication and consistent with standards set by the U.S. Food and Drug Administration and the general medical community. As medical research and practice advance, however, therapeutic standards may change. For this reason and because human and mechanical errors sometimes occur, we recommend that readers follow the advice of a physician who is directly involved in their care or the care of a member of their family.

Books published by the American Psychiatric Press, Inc., represent the views and opinions of the individual authors and do not necessarily represent the policies and opinions of the Press or the American Psychiatric Association.

Copyright © 1990 American Psychiatric Press, Inc.
ALL RIGHTS RESERVED
Manufactured in the United States of America
First Edition   93 92 91 90 4 3 2 1

The paper used in this publication meets the minimum requirements of the American National Standard for Information Sciences—Permanence of Paper for Printed Library Materials, ANSI Z39.48-1984.   ∞

Library of Congress Cataloging-in-Publication Data

Depression in schizophrenia / edited by Lynn E. Delisi.
        p.   cm.—(Progress in psychiatry)
    Based on the proceedings of a symposium held during the May 1986 Annual Meeting of the American Psychiatric Association.
    Includes bibliographies.
    ISBN 0-88048-196-X (alk. paper)
    1. Schizophrenia—Congresses. 2. Depression, Mental — Congresses. I. DeLisi, Lynn E. II. American Psychiatric Association. Meeting (139th : 1986 : Washington, D.C.) III. Series.
    [DNLM: 1. Depressive Disorder—congresses. 2. Schizophrenia—congresses. WM 203 D424 1986]
RC514.D37 1990
616.89'82—dc20
DNLM/DLC
for Library of Congress   89-15170
                                                     CIP

Contents

Contributors

Thomas Barnes, M.B.
Senior Lecturer in Psychiatry, Charing Cross and Westminster Medical School, London, United Kingdom

Timothy J. Crow, M.B., Ph.D.
Head, Division of Pyschiatry, Clinical Research Centre, Northwick Park Hospital, Harrow, Middlesex, United Kingdom

Lynn E. DeLisi, M.D.
Associate Professor, Department of Psychiatry, SUNY at Stony Brook, Stony Brook, New York

Steven R. Hirsch, M.D.
Professor and Head, Department of Psychiatry, Charing Cross and Westminster Medical School, London, United Kingdom

Anne L. Hoff, Ph.D.
Assistant Professor of Psychiatry, SUNY at Stony Brook, Stony Brook, New York

Anthony Jolley, M.B.
Consultant Psychiatrist, Charing Cross Hospital, London, United Kingdom

Julian Leff, Ph.D.
Professor and Head, Medical Research Council Psychiatry Unit, Friern Hospital, London, United Kingdom

Keith L. Rogers, M.D.
Assistant Professor of Psychiatry, University of Iowa College of Medicine, Iowa City, Iowa

Alec Roy, M.B.
Staff Psychiatrist, National Institute on Alcohol Abuse and Alcoholism, Bethesda, Maryland

Samuel G. Siris, M.D.
Director, Psychiatric Day Programs, Hillside Hospital, Division of the Long Island Jewish Medical Center, Brooklyn, New York

George Winokur, M.D.
Professor and Chairman, Department of Psychiatry, University of Iowa College of Medicine, Iowa City, Iowa

Introduction to the Progress in Psychiatry Series

The *Progress in Psychiatry* Series is designed to capture in print the excitement that comes from assembling a diverse group of experts from various locations to examine in detail the newest information about a developing aspect of psychiatry. This series emerged as a collaboration between the American Psychiatric Association's Scientific Program Committee and the American Psychiatric Press, Inc. Great interest was generated by a number of the symposia presented each year at the APA Annual Meeting, and we realized that much of the information presented there, carefully assembled by people who are deeply immersed in a given area, would unfortunately not appear together in print. The symposia sessions at the Annual Meetings provide an unusual opportunity for experts who otherwise might not meet on the same platform to share their diverse viewpoints for 3 hours. Some new themes are repeatedly reinforced and gain credence, while in other instances disagreements emerge, enabling the audience and now the reader to reach informed decisions about new directions in the field. The *Progress in Psychiatry* Series allows us to publish and capture some of the best of the symposia and thus provide an in-depth treatment of specific areas that might not oth-erwise be presented in broader review formats.

Psychiatry is by nature an interface discipline, combining the study of mind and brain, of individual and social environments, of the humane and the scientific. Therefore, progress in the field is rarely linear—it often comes from unexpected sources. Further, new developments emerge from an array of viewpoints that do not necessarily provide immediate agreement but rather expert examination of the issues. We intend to present innovative ideas and data that will enable you, the reader, to participate in this process.

We believe the *Progress in Psychiatry* Series will provide you with an opportunity to review timely new information in specific fields of interest as they are developing. We hope you find that the excitement of the presentations is captured in the written word and that this book proves to be informative and enjoyable reading.

David Spiegel, M.D.
Series Editor
Progress in Psychiatry Series

INTRODUCTION

M ost psychiatric diagnostic classifications do not include symptoms of depression as part of the clinical syndrome of schizophrenia, although patients with schizophrenia frequently complain of being "depressed," have several of the vegetative signs that occur with depression, may attempt suicide as part of their illness, and may be reclassified at some point in the lifetime of their disorder as having an affective disorder. The significance of this overlap with affective disorder is worth attention; it may be related to the biological etiology, at least in a subgroup of cases of schizophrenia, and may require specific pharmacological treatment.

The following symptoms, having a physiological-biochemical basis, are known to respond to pharmacotherapy and are used in the DSM-III (American Psychiatric Association 1980) diagnosis of major depressive disorder. Although these symptoms are often present in patients with the hallucinatory-delusional syndromes of schizophrenia, they are given minimal importance with respect to diagnosis, despite the possibility that they may have the same biological basis. These symptoms include loss of interest and pleasure in usual activities (apathy), psychomotor retardation or agitation, significant weight loss or weight gain due to appetite change, insomnia or hypersomnia, feelings of worthlessness, diminished ability to think, and recurrent thoughts of death. There is no diagnostic category for the postpsychotic depression that is often mentioned as common during the recovery phase of an acute psychotic episode or during exacerbation of schizophrenia, nor is there the recognition in our official diagnostic classification systems that depression may occur during all stages of psychotic illness. The biological mechanism for this occurrence has not been studied, and there is controversy about whether the use of antidepressant medication is warranted for these episodes when they occur as part of the schizophrenic syndrome. In addition, the symptoms of a true depressive episode have not been easily distinguished from side effects of neuroleptic medication and the negative symptoms of chronic schizophrenia.

It is, therefore, timely to address these important controversies in a unified volume about depression in schizophrenia, with chapters authored by investigators in the field who have contributed research and hypotheses toward a better understanding of this syndrome. This volume is based on the proceedings of a May 1986 American Psychiatric Association annual meeting symposium (Chicago) on "Depression and Schizophrenia," co-chaired by Professor Steven Hirsch and myself.

The prevalence of depression in patients with schizophrenia ranges from approximately 25% to 80%, depending on the stage of illness and mental state of the patient studied (Chapters 1 and 2). This significant number of cases warrants further inquiry into the biological basis and treatment of depression in schizophrenia.

Dr. Leff (Chapter 1) and Drs. Hirsch, Jolley, and Barnes (Chapter 2) review the literature on the characteristics and time course of depression in schizophrenia, as well as their own work in this field. They conclude that depression is an integral component of the schizophrenia illness, based on the often concurrent occurrence of clinical improvement of depression and psychosis. They suggest that the separate entity of "postpsychotic depression" is not clearly defined, since populations studied have been mixtures of patients with different time courses to their depressions, and thus probably different etiologies. These variables must be sorted out if treatment studies are to be useful.

Suicide is, of course, a permanent tragic consequence of our failure to produce symptom recovery to a degree in which life can be valued. Dr. Roy (Chapter 3) reviews the epidemiology of suicide, reasons for suicide, and its prediction in schizophrenia.

Chapter 4, by Drs. Rogers and Winokur; Chapter 5, by Dr. Crow; and Chapter 6, by Dr. Hoff and myself examine opposite ends of the controversial question of genetic overlap between schizophrenia and affective disorder, and whether these two major clinical disorders deserve independent classifications. If genetic vulnerabilities for schizophrenia and affective disorder are linked to independently sorting genes, then 1) increased prevalence of one syndrome in family members of persons with the other syndrome, 2) the occurrence of affective disorder in one monozygotic twin and schizophrenia in the other twin, and 3) the continuous nature of the boundaries between both illnesses (including the confusing schizoaffective diagnostic category) all must be explained. Contrary to popular thought, it may be that a common genetic defect leads to vulnerability for both syndromes and other nongenetic factors play a role in determining the clinical expression of the syndrome. The truth behind this controversy may eventually be uncovered when linkage to specific vulnerability genes is found and the extent of their clinical boundaries is examined in clinical studies within families. The present data to support or refute the above controversy and a comparison of clinical and biological genetic studies of both affective disorder and schizophrenia are reviewed in Chapter 6.

While the cause of depressive symptoms is an important area for future research, patients are in need of treatment now. In Chapter 7, Dr. Siris reviews the indications for specific pharmacotherapy for depression in schizophrenia, and how to proceed with antidepressant medication. He suggests that this treatment is particularly relevant to clear depression subsequent to psychosis, after neuroleptic stabilization, and when antiparkinsonian side effects have been controlled. Although these medications need not be widely used in schizophrenia and should not be prescribed on a long-term basis, careful consideration should be given to pharmacological alleviation of depression to prevent suicide attempts. Because our knowledge of the indications for specific types of antidepressant medications (tricyclics, monoamine oxidase inhibitors, and lithium) is limited, further research is needed.

Depression is an almost universal human emotion. When it is exaggerated and takes on the characteristics of a disease, it must be treated. It could be suggested that depression has many biological and nonbiological initiators, but that the pharmacological treatment may be similar regardless of etiology. Unless contraindicated, perhaps pharmacological treatment should be employed regardless of the primary illness present in each individual.

It is hoped that this volume will clarify some of the misperceptions that psychiatric researchers and clinicians have regarding depression in patients with schizophrenia.

I thank Ms. Angela Boccio for assistance in the preparation of this volume.

Lynn E. DeLisi, M.D.

REFERENCE

American Psychiatric Association: Diagnostic and Statistical Manual of Mental Disorders, Third Edition. Washington, DC, American Psychiatric Association, 1980

Chapter 1

Depressive Symptoms in the Course of Schizophrenia

Julian Leff, M.D.

Chapter 1

Depressive Symptoms in the Course of Schizophrenia

The dichotomy established by Kraepelin between schizophrenia and manic-depressive illness has had the effect of polarizing the concepts of these conditions held by psychiatrists. The boundary between them has fluctuated in position over the years, particularly in the United States where it used to define a broad category of schizophrenia and a narrow category of affective illness (Cooper et al. 1972) whereas now the situation is reversed (American Psychiatric Association 1980). The mutual exclusivity of these categories is implicit in most classificatory systems, although the recognition of "schizoaffective psychosis," by DSM-III (American Psychiatric Association 1980), for example, is an acknowledgment of overlap across the boundary. However, the existence of this category, which is used relatively seldom by clinicians, does not do justice to the frequency with which affective symptoms occur in schizophrenic illnesses. Kraepelin himself observed that "it is common to find cases of undeniable schizophrenia which show transitory or at times long-lasting manic-depressive symptoms" (Kraepelin 1974, p. 28).

In recent years, a renewed interest in the relationship of depressive symptoms to schizophrenia appears to have arisen as a consequence of the development of standardized assessments of the mental state, such as the Brief Psychiatric Rating Scale (Overall and Gorham 1962) and the Present State Examination (PSE) (Wing et al. 1974). In routine clinical practice there is an understandable tendency to cut corners in examining the patient's psychiatric state, particularly under pressure of work. Once the interviewer has established to his or her satisfaction that definitive symptoms of schizophrenia are present, the interviewer is unlikely to proceed with an exhaustive inquiry into the full range of possible symptoms. However, a semistructured interview schedule impels the interviewer to cover the whole range of psychopathology. Such research tools became an integral component of drug trials and of international comparative studies.

3

One of the earliest studies to detect depression in schizophrenic patients using a standardized interview was conducted by Bowers and Astrachan (1967), who were stimulated to make serial ratings of symptoms by "the appearance and persistence of depression in the course of some acute psychoses treated with phenothiazines" (p. 976). They did not employ a very sophisticated instrument, but required residents to make weekly ratings on 9-point scales of five psychotic symptoms and five depressive symptoms. No attempt was made to establish the interrater reliability of these assessments. They studied a sample of 36 patients admitted to their facility with "an unequivocal diagnosis of schizophrenic reaction made at discharge" (p. 976). Of these patients, 20 were admitted for the first time; 16 were readmissions. All were treated with phenothiazines, 16 were given antidepressants in addition, and 3 received electroconvulsive therapy (ECT). Among the patients who received no treatment for depression, it was noted that ratings for depression followed those for psychosis rather closely. This led the authors to conclude "either that the clinical picture during hospitalization did not lend itself to a clear-cut separation of the two behaviors by the rater or that the depressive behavior was improved by phenothiazines alone" (p. 977). They noted additionally that on follow-up 3 first admission patients who did not manifest depression while in hospital suffered marked depressive reactions following discharge while still receiving phenothiazines.

By contrast, the patients who received some form of antidepressant treatment showed an increase in ratings of depression after a major improvement had occurred in psychotic symptoms. The authors did not find any significant change in the depression ratings after the institution of antidepressant treatment, and concluded that this did not appear to be effective.

This early study raised a number of issues that have continued to dominate research in this area. Are depressive symptoms an integral part of acute schizophrenic illnesses or are they a consequence of treatment with neuroleptic drugs? What is the nature of depressive episodes occurring after the schizophrenic illness has abated? What treatment is indicated for depression in patients suffering from schizophrenia? I shall attempt to present the evidence relevant to these questions in this chapter, although definitive answers are not yet available.

EARLY FINDINGS

A concern that antipsychotic treatment might itself produce or worsen depression developed soon after the introduction of reserpine into psychiatric practice. Reserpine had already been noted to induce depression in patients receiving it as treatment for hypertension (Freis 1954), so that it is not surprising that this effect gave rise to serious problems when the drug was used for treating schizophrenia. In particular, the suicidal behavior of psychiatric patients treated with reserpine aroused such alarm that the drug was rapidly ousted by chlorpromazine soon after the use of the latter was adopted by psychiatrists. It is possible that the eclipse of rauwolfia was not justified on the grounds of its depressogenic qualities, since even at the time Ayd (1958) questioned the interpretation of psychiatrists' observations. He considered that in some patients depression had existed prior to treatment but had not been diagnosed, whereas in others the lethargy, anergy, and psychomotor retardation induced by reserpine were misperceived as depression. As will be seen, exactly the same queries arise in respect to the depression supposedly induced by the phenothiazines that supplanted reserpine.

POSTPSYCHOTIC DEPRESSION

To return to studies using standardized clinical assessment, the report of Bowers and Astrachan (1967) was closely paralleled by an article published in the same year by Steinberg et al. (1967). A similar clinical observation impelled Steinberg et al. to initiate their research, namely: "in the course of treating patients with acute schizophrenic episodes, we have been impressed with the frequency with which significant depression of mood occurs in the period following remission of overtly psychotic symptoms" (p. 699). Like Bowers and Astrachan, they employed a weekly rating scale completed by the ward physician. In this instance, they introduced two 7-point scales to assess overall psychotic behavior and depressed mood. From the ward admissions they selected patients who had psychotic symptoms severe enough to be rated 5 or above on the psychotic scale and whose ratings fell to 2 or below during a 6-week period. Unfortunately, only 8 of 41 patients met these criteria, all of them receiving phenothiazine drugs during their stay on the ward. For the whole group of 8, ratings of depression during the 6 weeks of remission were significantly higher than for the rest of the hospital stay. There was considerable variation within this group, however, with some patients showing persistently high ratings on depression for many weeks while others had a single high rating. Furthermore, several of the remitted patients had their highest depression ratings during the period of acute psychosis. The authors raise the possibility that the depression might be a result of phenothiazine treatment, but they are unable to throw any light on the question with their study design.

The one conclusion that can be drawn from the small sample of patients they studied is that depression emerging during an acute episode of schizophrenia is likely to be heterogeneous in nature.

A much larger group of patients was studied by Shanfield et al. (1970), who also included a comparison sample of depressed patients. They inducted into the study consecutive admissions who were judged by two experienced clinicians to be suffering from schizophrenia (n = 44), psychotic depression (n = 18), or neurotic depression (n = 18). Like Bowers and Astrachan (1967), they used 9-point rating scales, but asked nurses in addition to psychiatrists to fill out the scales. They stated that the scales had been shown to have satisfactory interrater reliability. Psychiatrists completed the scales at weeks 1, 3, 7, and 10; nurses' ratings over a 3-day period were averaged at the same time points. In addition, the patients filled out a selection of self-rating questionnaires including the Zung Self-Rating Depressive Scale (Zung 1965).

On admission, the psychiatrists rated the depressed patients as being significantly more depressed than the schizophrenic patients, and the patients' self-report, although not the nurses' ratings, confirmed this. Over the 10-week period of observation, there was a marked decline in almost all the symptoms of the various diagnostic groups. However, the depressive symptomatology of the diagnosed depressives decreased at a much more rapid rate than that of the schizophrenic patients, and by the 10th week the former tended to be less depressed than the latter. Study of individual cases revealed that only one schizophrenic patient who showed little depression at week 1 was markedly depressed at week 7. The overwhelming majority (93%) of the schizophrenic group were treated with phenothiazine medication, leading Shanfield et al. (1970) to conclude that this is unlikely to be the cause of the depression observed since depressive symptomatology decreased over time. Instead they favor the explanation that "depressive symptoms [are] present from the onset of the schizophrenic episode, which apparently remain unnoticed until the remission of the more bizarre and noteworthy psychotic symptoms" (p. 209). They believe that the depressive symptoms achieved recognition in their sample because "the psychiatrists were forced to rate specifically and routinely for this factor" (p. 209). Their conclusion that depressive symptoms form an important part of the symptom complex for some schizophrenic patients must be somewhat tempered by the fact that they failed to state whether any of the patients were receiving phenothiazine medication *before* admission to their facility.

Stern et al. (1972) investigated the same problem, which they labeled "postpsychotic depression," a term that has been used for a variety of different phenomena as will be discussed later. They studied 17 recently admitted patients with a ward diagnosis of schizophrenia, in whom affective and psychotic symptoms had been present for less than 6 months. All but one of the patients were Black. The patients were rated over a 6-month period with the authors' own structured instrument: The Profile for Rating Depressive and Schizophrenic Behavior. The ratings were made three times a week for the first week and then progressively less frequently down to once a month toward the end of the follow-up period. From the profile, 4 schizophrenic items and 5 depressive items were selected, each being scored on a 0 to 3 scale. Nine of the 17 patients showed no depression at any time, 5 scored a significant rating at some time while they were still psychotic, while the remaining 3 developed depression anew after the resolution of their psychosis. In one patient this was very brief and mild, only being recorded during 1 week. The other 2 patients experienced moderate and severe depression lasting several weeks or more. All but one of the sample received antipsychotic drugs. The authors were surprised by the relatively small proportions of patients developing postpsychotic depression, but this is confirmed by later, more sophisticated studies. Their surprise is probably to be understood in terms of the explanation proposed by Shanfield et al. (1970) that what is commonly referred to in the literature as post-psychotic depression has been present, unnoticed, throughout the psychosis.

Findings of the International Pilot Study of Schizophrenia

Confirmation of this proposition is provided on an international scale by the International Pilot Study of Schizophrenia (IPSS) (World Health Organization 1973). This collaborative study involved nine centers distributed over five developed and four developing countries. In all, 1,202 patients were included, of whom 811 received a center diagnosis of schizophrenia. A standardized clinical examination was conducted using the PSE, which was translated from English into the seven other languages used in the centers. Very few patients in any of the centers were so agitated or otherwise difficult to interview that they could not be evaluated with the PSE within the first few days of their admission. The PSE in its ninth edition comprises 140 items condensed into 38 syndromes. In this chapter I will be particularly concerned with the syndromes that include depressive items. The four relevant syndromes are shown in Table 1.

The research psychiatrists in each center were required to make a diagnosis on each patient in terms of categories in the International

Classification of Diseases (ICD). It was found that seven of the centers were in close agreement in their use of the term *schizophrenia*. However, psychiatrists in Washington and Moscow were employing it for a considerably broader spread of patients, including a proportion who would have been diagnosed as affective disorders in the other centers. With this proviso, it is possible to group the patients across all nine centers according to ICD categories. This has been done in Table 2, which shows the proportion of patients in each major diagnostic category who exhibited one of the "depressive" syndromes.

It is noteworthy that the profile of typical schizophrenic patients for these depressive syndromes is not very different from that of patients with neurotic depression. Thus an international comparison across widely differing cultural groups reinforces the findings from American studies that schizophrenic patients exhibit a multiplicity of depressive symptoms on or shortly after admission. Once more,

Table 1. "Depressive" Present State Examination Syndromes

Syndrome	Item no.	Item
Depressive delusions and hallucinations	61	Depressive hallucinations
	88	Delusions of guilt
	91	Hypochondriacal delusions
	92	Delusions of catastrophe
Simple depression	19	Subjectively inefficient thinking
	23	Subjective complaint of depression
	24	Hopelessness
	25	Suicidal plans or acts
	121	Observed depression
Special symptoms of depression	29	Self-depreciation
	32	Guilty ideas of reference
	33	Pathological guilt
	51	Dulled perception
	54	Lost affect
Other symptoms of depression	34	Loss of weight
	37	Early waking
	38	Loss of libido

however, a shadow lies over the interpretation of these observations, since an unknown proportion of the schizophrenic patients in the IPSS were already receiving antipsychotic drugs when the PSE was carried out.

Longitudinal Studies of Depression in Schizophrenic Patients

The frequency with which schizophrenic patients exhibit depression in the acute phase of the illness was also emphasized by McGlashan and Carpenter (1976). They selected 30 patients from a National Institute of Mental Health program, who were assessed with the Psychiatric Assessment Interview, a structured clinical interview based on the PSE. The sample was subdivided into 15 who were depressed at or just after discharge, and 15 who showed no depression during the same period. Comparison of the two groups revealed no significant differences with respect to sex, ethnic origin, marital status, social class, or diagnosis. Scores from the Psychiatric Assessment Interview on a depressive dimension were calculated for three assessments: during the first 3 weeks of hospitalization, before discharge, and at a 1-year follow-up. It was found that both groups of patients were equally depressed initially, but that depression remitted more slowly for the 15 patients who scored as depressed just before discharge.

McGlashan and Carpenter (1976) also investigated the relationship between depressive symptoms and neuroleptic drugs. It was the practice in their unit to remove patients from all medication for the first 3 weeks. Subsequently, 9 of the 15 patients in the depressed

Table 2.   "Depressive" Present State Examination Syndromes in Four ICD Diagnostic Groups

ICD diagnosis	n	Syndrome present %			
		DD	ED	OD	SD
"Typical" schizophrenia	588	15	39	78	81
Mania	79	8	19	76	52
Depressive psychosis	73	34	59	96	97
Depressive neurosis	70	10	42	94	99

Note. ICD = International Classification of Diseases; DD = depressive delusions and hallucinations; ED = special symptoms of depression; OD = other symptoms of depression; SD = simple depression. Adapted from World Health Organization (1973).

group received a phenothiazine compared with 4 of the 15 nondepressed patients, a nonsignificant difference. In a later article, Carpenter et al. (1977) reported on a larger group of 49 schizophrenic patients from the same program. After a 3-week period of medication, 22 patients of this group were treated with phenothiazines, whereas the remaining 27 continued to be cared for without drugs. It was found that the two subgroups had been equally depressed initially, but the patients prescribed phenothiazines were significantly more likely to be rated as depressed before discharge. There is a suggestion from these findings that depression continuing after psychotic symptoms have remitted, termed *postpsychotic depression* by McGlashan and Carpenter (1976), may be partly attributable to treatment with phenothiazines. Although all the patients in these studies were off medication when assessed initially, one cannot be certain that the depression present at that time was unrelated to phenothiazine drugs since the patients had been withdrawn from their medication for a maximum of 3 weeks, insufficient time for the possible effects of phenothiazines to have dissipated.

A different view of postpsychotic depression was taken by Mandel et al. (1982). They studied 211 schizophrenic patients who participated in a trial of two depot antipsychotic drugs. The patients were assessed with the Brief Psychiatric Rating Scale (BPRS) (Overall and Gorham 1962) and the Hamilton Depression Scale (HDS) (Hamilton 1960). They were followed through from admission to discharge, when they were judged to be free of depression in that they scored less than "moderate" on the depressive mood item of the BPRS. During the year after discharge, about 25% of the patients exceeded the threshold score of 16 on the HDS and were therefore considered to be significantly depressed. For the majority of patients, depression emerged between 3 to 5 months after discharge. It is evident that Mandel et al. used the term *postpsychotic depression* to refer to a much longer time scale than in any of the earlier published work. By mounting a long-term follow-up of a large group of patients, Mandel et al. were able to examine the relationship of postpsychotic depression to the subsequent course of schizophrenia. They found that patients who developed depression after discharge were more likely to relapse or to be rehospitalized than the nondepressed group.

This issue was also investigated by Johnson (1988) using the HDS as well as other assessment instruments. He studied a sample of 80 chronic schizophrenic patients, all of whom were maintained on long-acting depot injections for the whole of a 3-year follow-up period. He defined postpsychotic depression as "depression occurring within

12 months of the patient recovering from an acute episode of illness" (p. 321). Depression that occurred at other times during the study was termed *nonpostpsychotic depression*. The criteria for the presence of depression were a duration of at least 7 days, scores above threshold on the HDS or the Beck Depression Inventory (Beck et al. 1961), and meeting the DSM-III criteria for depression. Relapse of schizophrenia was defined in terms of scores on the BPRS. Johnson found that the risk of schizophrenic relapse over the 3-year follow-up was significantly higher for patients with nonpostpsychotic depression than for those with postpsychotic depression or those with no depression ($p < .001$). This result is at variance with that of Mandel et al. (1982), but this may be because Johnson studied only chronic patients and followed up the sample for a much longer period. Johnson pointed out that depression occurring after a year free of symptoms, in many cases, constitutes the first symptom of a new episode of schizophrenia. In these instances, it would be tautological to refer to depression as predicting subsequent relapse of schizophrenia.

A number of recent studies have included standardized assessment of schizophrenic patients on admission and during treatment with neuroleptic drugs. Knights and Hirsch (1981) interviewed 27 acute schizophrenic patients with the PSE a week after admission, and then 3 months later. They compared them with a group of 62 patients with a variety of types of depression who went through the same procedure. All the schizophrenic patients were treated with neuroleptic drugs during their admission and all the depressed patients received antidepressant drugs. Depressive syndromes (see Table 1) were present in about two-thirds of the schizophrenic patients on admission and showed a very similar distribution to those in the depressed patients. The schizophrenic group exhibited a significant ($p < .001$) reduction in depressive symptoms after 3 months of neuroleptic treatment. However, this group effect concealed a reverse trend in a few patients. Three patients (11%) showed an increase in depressive scores at 3 months compared with their assessment on admission; one patient (4%) had a rating of 0 at first assessment and developed depressive symptoms by the 3-month follow-up. These findings suggest that while the majority of schizophrenic patients experience a relief from depression as their psychosis subsides, a small proportion exhibit an increase in depression or its appearance de novo. It is in these that the possibility of neuroleptic-induced depression needs to be seriously considered.

Similar results to those of Knights and Hirsch (1981) were obtained by Siris et al. (1987), who studied 20 patients satisfying Research Diagnostic Criteria (RDC) for schizophrenia after 1 week in the hospital. The patients were rated at weekly intervals until discharge with an abbreviated version of the Schedule for Affective Disorders and Schizophrenia (SADS) (Endicott and Spitzer 1978). Of the 20 patients, 17 met DSM-III criteria for schizophrenia and the remainder satisfied the criteria for schizophreniform disorder. All patients were treated with neuroleptic drugs, and most received antiparkinsonian drugs. None were prescribed antidepressants. Depressive syndromes satisfying RDC were recorded in two patients during the first week, in three in the second week, two in the third week, and one in the fourth week of rating. Therefore, eight (40%) in all developed depressive syndromes during the first month of hospitalization. One patient (5%) developed a syndrome equivalent to a major depression after the symptoms of psychosis had almost entirely subsided, while 3 (15%) additional patients developed minor depressive syndromes after psychotic symptoms had entirely or almost entirely resolved. These rates are very similar to those of Knights and Hirsch (1981).

Hogarty and Munetz (1984) investigated the problem by retrospective analysis of data from a placebo-controlled trial of chlorpromazine. They found that 6 (10%) of 60 drug patients and 4 (15%) of 27 placebo patients who were judged not depressed 2 months into the trial met narrow criteria for depression at 6 months. These results weigh against chlorpromazine as a factor in postpsychotic depression.

The largest scale study on this topic was conducted by Möller and Von Zerssen (1985), whose sample comprised 280 inpatients with a diagnosis of schizophrenia. Patients with schizoaffective psychosis were excluded. These authors employed a comparison group of inpatients suffering from acute endogenous depression, and performed assessments with the Inpatient Multidimensional Psychiatric Schedule (IMPS). The schizophrenic and depressed patients were found to have similarly high scores at admission on "anxious depression," "retardation and apathy," and "impaired functioning." At discharge, both groups showed an equivalent reduction in the scores on these three syndromes, although the schizophrenic patients received neuroleptic drugs and the depressed patients were prescribed antidepressants. Despite this general improvement, a small proportion of schizophrenic patients (5 to 10%) were more depressed at discharge than at admission, a finding consonant with the results of the two preceding studies.

These data were augmented with a self-rating mood scale, which patients were required to complete every other day. A depressive period was defined as at least three consecutive self-ratings, each totaling more than 21. Only 14% of all schizophrenic patients developed such a depressive period without also having abnormal mood scores on admission.

Möller and Von Zerssen (1985) also looked at the ability of depressive symptoms to predict the long-term outcome of schizophrenia. They followed up their sample of patients for 5 years and found that poor outcome was unrelated to the "anxious depression" scores on the IMPS or to self-ratings of depression. This is closer to the finding of Johnson (1988) than to that of Mandel et al. (1982), although comparison across studies is hampered by the fact that depression was measured at a different point in the course of the illness in each of them.

First Episodes of Schizophrenia and Depressive Syndromes

Another large sample, studied by House et al. (1987), had the unusual characteristics of being epidemiologically based and comprising only first episodes of schizophrenia. One of the aims of this study was to determine whether depressed mood occurring in schizophrenic patients might be a variant of an extrapyramidal syndrome, designated "akinetic depression" by Van Putten and May (1978). The sample consisted of 68 subjects given a definite diagnosis of schizophrenia by two or more experienced psychiatrists. Clinical assessment was by means of the PSE. A "total depression score" was defined as the sum of scores for the three syndromes: simple depression, special symptoms of depression, and other symptoms of depression (see Table 1). A syndrome of akinesia was derived from certain behavioral items included in the PSE.

At onset, 15 of the 68 patients (22%) were defined as depressed cases in that they achieved a total depression score of 5 or more in the presence of depressed mood. Twenty-one patients (31%) had some score on the other symptoms of depression syndrome. There was no significant association between any of the depressive syndromes and akinesia, indicating that these phenomena can be reliably distinguished from each other.

It proved possible to complete a follow-up interview at 1 year on 56 of the original sample. Over this period there was a decrease in prevalence of the depressive syndromes. In particular, only five patients were defined as depressed cases at follow-up; three of these had been definite and one a borderline case at onset. By contrast, akinesia became more prevalent by 1 year follow-up and was significantly associated with neuroleptic treatment.

House et al. (1987) concluded that a wide range of depressive symptoms were present at the first onset of schizophrenia and were generally unrelated to concurrent neuroleptic medication. They point out, however, that the lapse of a year between the two clinical assessments does not preclude the possibility of a brief but major depressive episode emerging undetected and resolving spontaneously. The patients who were found to be depressed at follow-up were largely the same individuals who were depressed at onset; few new cases of depression emerged at follow-up. Moreover, the prevalence of depression decreased with time, whereas the opposite tendency was seen with akinesia, which was associated with the taking of neuroleptics.

Johnson (1985) also studied a group of first onset schizophrenic patients, but used the HDS and the Beck Depression Inventory for assessment. He found that 37% of the patients gave a history of recent depression, while 19% exhibited depression at the time of examination. He also assessed a group of schizophrenic patients who had relapsed after discontinuing medication, and found depression to be present in 30%.

Studies of Unmedicated Schizophrenic Patients

Our own study (Leff et al. 1988) adds to the existing literature in that we focused on schizophrenic patients who had either never received neuroleptic drugs or had been free of them for some time and in that we charted the weekly course of all symptoms present on admission. For this purpose we employed a modified version of the PSE known as the PSE Change Rating Scale (Tress et al. 1987). The items scored as present on the initial PSE were used as a basis for change ratings, which were made weekly by a psychiatrist trained to a high level of reliability in the use of this instrument. The interview has been developed to provide a sensitive assessment of clinical change and to avoid halo effects in rating. Each PSE item is scored on an 8-point scale, the midpoint 4 representing no change. After the initial assessment, most items remained unchanged or improved to a greater or lesser extent. It was rare for any item to show worsening in the period following admission.

The sample consisted of 31 patients, 16 of whom were admitted for the first time with a schizophrenic illness and had not previously received neuroleptic drugs. The majority of the remainder had been off such medication for a number of months. Once the diagnosis of schizophrenia had been made, patients were started on a standard regime of oral haloperidol. This consisted of an initial dose of 3 mg twice daily for the first week, which was increased by 3 mg twice daily every week, in stepwise fashion, until the patient's mental state stabilized. Following stabilization on oral haloperidol, patients were transferred to an equivalent dose of long-acting haloperidol decanoate.

On admission, when the patients were free of drugs, 14 (45%) of the 31 were rated positive on depressed mood. Each of the depressive syndromes from the PSE (see Table 1) was deemed to be present if any one constituent item was rated positively. Simple depression was present in 19 (61%), special symptoms of depression in 7 (23%), and other symptoms of depression in 10 (32%).

In analyzing the relationship between the course of schizophrenic and depressive symptoms, it was decided to concentrate on depressed mood (item 23 of PSE), since this is the central feature of depressive conditions. For 1 of the 14 patients with depressed mood rated initially, the change ratings of this item were omitted by mistake. However, one patient without depressed mood on admission developed this symptom at week 14 and has been included in the analysis. The change ratings for total psychotic symptoms, depressed mood, and three of the depressive PSE syndromes—simple depression, special symptoms of depression, and other symptoms of depression—(see Table 1) were plotted for each of the 14 patients. In the majority of cases, the psychotic ratings showed a very similar pattern to the various depressive ratings. To express this relationship statistically, the product-moment correlation between mean change rating on total psychotic symptoms and depressed mood was calculated for each patient.

The correlation coefficient ranged from -0.08 to 0.98; however, in only four patients was it below 0.50. In one of these patients there was virtually no change in the ratings of psychotic symptoms (range, 3.4 to 4.0) or of depressed mood (range, 3.6 to 4.0) so that the low value of r gives a false impression of a discrepancy in their clinical course. The other three patients are of particular interest and will be discussed in detail below. In the remaining 10 patients, the value of r ranged from 0.53 to 0.98, with a mean of 0.78. Including the patient in whom neither set of symptoms altered much, 11 of the 14 patients showed a considerable similarity in the clinical course of schizophrenic symptoms and depressed mood. When schizophrenic symptoms declined in response to the neuroleptic regime, depressed mood attenuated over the same time period. When medication made little or no impact on schizophrenic symptoms, depressed mood also continued unchanged. A representative set of ratings is displayed in Figure 1. For this patient, r between psychotic symptoms and depressed mood was 0.83.

Of the three patients in whom the course of the two types of symptoms were discrepant, two developed depressed mood for the first time some weeks after admission. In one patient, the psychotic symptoms had already subsided, while in the other they continued unchanged throughout 29 weeks of rating. The third patient lost all psychotic symptoms after 10 weeks of treatment, and, at about the same time, depressed mood, which was present from admission,

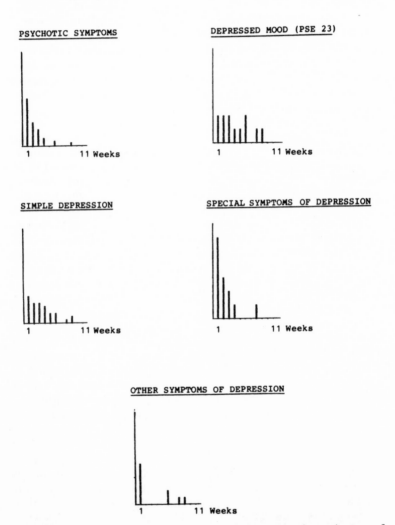

Figure 1. Present State Examination change ratings for patient no. 1. *Horizontal axis*: time in weeks. *Vertical axis*: change rating score 0 to 7.

showed a considerable worsening that continued for some weeks, then ameliorated.

We concluded that the whole spectrum of depressive symptoms is present in varying proportions of drug-free acutely ill schizophrenic patients, and that in the majority of these, psychotic symptoms and depressive symptoms run a very similar time course. In a small minority, however, depressive symptoms either outlast the resolution of psychotic symptoms or appear for the first time as the psychotic symptoms fade. We cannot tell from our study whether these two varieties of postpsychotic depression are attributable to neuroleptic medication or not, since every patient received this treatment.

CONCLUSIONS

Our conclusions also apply to this review of the literature, the key studies of which are summarized in Table 3 for ease of comparison. Depressive symptoms of various kinds have been found in schizophrenic patients when assessed on admission, the proportion ranging from 19% (Johnson 1985) to 81% (World Health Organization 1973). This variation in proportion results partly from the particular depressive symptoms measured and partly from whether the patients are in an acute or a chronic phase of the illness. When psychotic and depressive symptoms have been charted over time, in the majority of schizophrenic patients studied, they have run the same course. In virtually every study of this nature, the patients have been prescribed neuroleptic drugs, but not antidepressants. These facts taken together constitute strong evidence for regarding depressive symptoms as an integral part of a schizophrenic illness.

This notion was put forward earlier by Foulds and Bedford (1975), who developed a theoretical schema describing the interrelationship of psychiatric symptoms. A modified form of this schema is shown in Figure 2. The schema is organized hierarchically, with the implication that a patient exhibiting symptoms at any particular level should also show symptoms pertaining to each of the lower levels. For example, a patient with specific neurotic symptoms, such as phobic anxiety or depression, would be expected to complain in addition of nonspecific symptoms, such as worrying, tension headaches, or irritability. A patient with schizophrenia should always exhibit symptoms of affective psychoses, such as grandiose delusions, as well as specific neurotic symptoms and nonspecific neurotic symptoms. Patients with affective psychoses, at the third level of the hierarchy, should show specific and nonspecific neurotic symptoms, as well as delusions and hallucinations of an affective type. A number of studies have shown that a high proportion of acute and chronic patients (75% to 96%) show patterns of symptoms that do conform to Foulds and Bedford's schema. The most recent of these (Morey 1985) involved 52 long-stay inpatients in Yale Psychiatric Institute. The degree of concordance with the model was found to be 90%, a better fit than with models based on severity of disturbance and prevalence. In view of the empirical support for Foulds and Bedford's diagnostic schema, it deserves more attention from the psychiatric community than it has attracted to date. Incidentally, it is worth noting that the schema makes the category of schizoaffective psychosis redundant.

Table 3. Studies in Which Depressive and Schizophrenic Symptoms Were Measured at Admission and/or Follow-Up

Reference	Patients N	Patients with depression initially		Follow-up period (months)	Patients with depression after resolution of psychosis	
		n	%		*n*	%
Shanfield et al. (1970)	17	5	29	6	3	18
World Health Organization (1973)	588	476	81	—	—	
Mandel et al. (1982)	211	—		12	47	22
Knights and Hirsch (1981)	27	18	67	3	4	15
Hogarty and Munetz (1984)	87	—		6	10	11
Siris et al. (1987)	20	8	40	1	4	20
Möller and Von Zerssen (1985)	280	—		to discharge	39	14
House et al. (1987)	68	15	22	12	5[a]	9
Johnson (1985)	37	7	19	—	—	
Leff et al. (1988)	31	14	45	1–7	3	10

[a]Out of 56 followed up.

Finally we need to consider those patients in whom the course of depressive symptoms is not in accord with that of psychotic symptoms. These constitute a small proportion of the samples studied, ranging from 9% to 22%, with a mean of 15%. The term *postpsychotic depression* has been used for these patients, but there are at least three types of clinical course, as shown in Figure 3.

In describing the clinical features of postpsychotic depression,

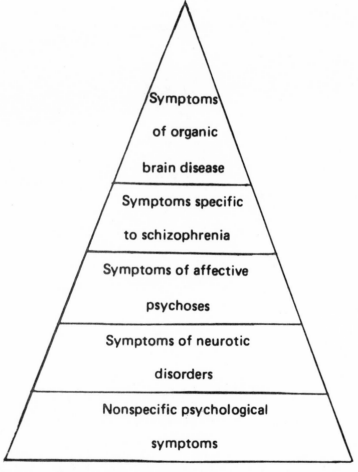

Figure 2. The hierarchical schema of psychiatric symptoms. Adapted from Foulds and Bedford (1975).

McGlashan and Carpenter (1976) were clearly referring to Type A: "Depression was commonly present for both groups during the acute phase of psychosis and remitted over time along with the rest of the psychotic pathology but the depressive picture remitted more slowly for patients who were postpsychotically depressed" (p. 16). On the other hand, Stern et al. (1972) used the term for a mixture of Types A and B, whereas Mandel et al. (1982) included only patients whose depression appeared during the year following discharge (Type C). It is quite likely that the clinical heterogeneity of samples studied under this rubric has given rise to the conflicting results on prediction of outcome (Johnson 1988; Mandel et al. 1982) and on the response

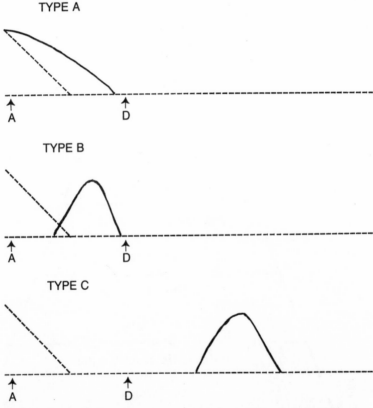

Figure 3.   Three types of clinical course in postpsychotic depression. A = admission; D = discharge; *broken line* = psychotic symptoms; *solid line* = depressive symptoms.

of depression in schizophrenic patients to antidepressant drugs (Johnson 1981; Siris et al. 1987). It is necessary to clarify the diagnostic status of these three types of depression and their relationship to one another. The problem should yield to epidemiological studies of prevalence of these types, observations of their natural history, and studies of their response to antidepressant and antipsychotic treatments.

REFERENCES

American Psychiatric Association: Diagnostic and Statistical Manual of Mental Disorders, Third Edition. Washington, DC, American Psychiatric Association, 1980

Ayd FJ: Drug-induced depression: fact or fallacy. NY State J Med 58:354–356, 1958

Beck AT, Ward CH, Mendelsohn I, et al: An inventory for measuring depression. Arch Gen Psychiatry 4:561–571, 1961

Bowers MB, Astrachan BM: Depression in acute schizophrenic psychosis. Am J Psychiatry 123:976–979, 1967

Carpenter WT, McGlashan TH, Strauss JS: The treatment of acute schizophrenia without drugs: an investigation of some current assumptions. Am J Psychiatry 134:14–20, 1977

Cooper JE, Kendell RE, Gurland BJ, et al: Psychiatric Diagnosis in New York and London: Maudsley Monograph No. 20. Oxford University Press, London, 1972

Endicott J, Spitzer RL: A diagnostic interview: The Schedule for Affective Disorders and Schizophrenia. Arch Gen Psychiatry 35:837–844, 1978

Foulds GA, Bedford A: Hierarchy of classes of personal illness. Psychol Med 5:181–192, 1975

Freis ED: Mental depression in hypertensive patients treated for long periods with large doses of reserpine. N Engl J Med 251:1006–1008, 1954

Hamilton M: A rating scale for depression. J Neurol Neurosurg Psychiatry 23:56–62, 1960

Hogarty GE, Munetz MR: Pharmacogenic depression among outpatient schizophrenic patients: a failure to substantiate. J Clin Psychopharm 4:17–24, 1984

House A, Bostock J, Cooper J: Depressive syndromes in the year following onset of a first schizophrenic illness. Br J Psychiatry 151:773–779, 1987

Johnson DAW: A double-blind trial of nortriptyline for depression in chronic schizophrenia. Br J Psychiatry 139:97–101, 1981

Johnson DAW: Some observations on the frequency of depression in schizophrenia, in Psychiatry: The State of the Art, Vol 1. Edited by Pichaud P, Berner P, Wolfe R, Thau K. New York, Plenum Press, 1985, pp 589–593

Johnson DAW: The significance of depression in the prediction of relapse in chronic schizophrenia. Br J Psychiatry 152:320–323, 1988

Knights A, Hirsch SR: "Revealed" depression and drug treatment for schizophrenia. Arch Gen Psychiatry 38:806–811, 1981

Kraepelin E: Patterns of mental disorder, in Themes and Variations in European Psychiatry: An Anthology. Edited by Hirsch SR, Shepherd M. Bristol, John Wright & Sons, 1974

Leff J, Tress K, Edwards B: The clinical course of depressive symptoms in schizophrenia. Schizophrenia Research 1: 25–30, 1988

Mandel MR, Severe JB, Schooler NR, et al: Development and prediction of post-psychotic depression in neuroleptic-treated schizophrenic. Arch Gen Psychiatry 39:197–203, 1982

McGlashan TH, Carpenter WT: An investigation of the postpsychotic depressive syndrome. Am J Psychiatry 133:14–19, 1976

Möller HJ, Von Zerssen D: The nature of the depressive syndrome in schizophrenia and its relationship to prognosis, in Psychological Measurements in Psychopharmacology Vol 7, Modern Problems in Pharmacopsychiatry. Edited by Pichaud P, Olivier R. Basel, Karger, 1985

Morey LC: A comparative validation of the Foulds and Bedford Hierarchy of psychiatric symptomatology. Br J Psychiatry 14:424–428, 1985

Overall JE, Gorham DR: The Brief Psychiatric Rating Scale. Psychol Reports 10:799–812, 1962

Shanfield S, Tucker GJ, Harrow M, et al: The schizophrenic patient and depressive symptomatology. J Nerv Ment Dis 151:203–210, 1970

Siris SG, Morgan V, Fagerstrom R, et al: Adjunctive imipramine in the treatment of postpsychotic depression. Arch Gen Psychiatry 44:533–539, 1987

Steinberg AR, Green R, Durrell J: Depression occurring during the course of recovery from schizophrenic symptoms. Am J Psychiatry 124:699–702, 1967

Stern MJ, Pillsbury JA, Sonnenberg SM: Postpsychotic depression in schizophrenics. Compr Psychiatry 13:591–598, 1972

Tress KH, Bellenis C, Brownlow JM, et al: The Present State Examination Change Rating Scale. Br J Psychiatry 150:201–207, 1987

Van Putten T, May P: "Akinetic depression" in schizophrenia. Arch Gen Psychiatry 35:1101–1107, 1978

Wing JK, Cooper JE, Sartorius N: The Measurement and Classification of Psychiatric Symptoms. London, Cambridge University Press, 1974

World Health Organization: The International Pilot Study of Schizophrenia, Vol 1. Geneva, World Health Organization, 1973

Zung WWK: A self rating depression scale. Arch Gen Psychiatry 12:63–70, 1965

Chapter 2

Are Depressive Symptoms Part of the Schizophrenic Syndrome?

Steven R. Hirsch, M.D.
Anthony Jolley, M.B.
Thomas Barnes, M.B.

Chapter 2

Are Depressive Symptoms Part of the Schizophrenic Syndrome?

PREVIOUS WORK

We have been interested in the high prevalence of depressive syndromes in schizophrenic patients for about 20 years and first published in 1973 (Hirsch et al. 1973). It is as well to remind ourselves, however, that both Kraepelin and Bleuler were well aware of the problem more than 80 years ago. In the same article where he first introduced the term *schizophrenia* in 1908, Bleuler demonstrated his awareness of the problem when he wrote:

> The special position of depressive mood swings in schizophrenia varies from case to case and in some cases seems to be triggered by the schizophrenic disease process, and in others takes on the role of secondary symptoms which have their origin in the basic schizophrenic process, although rarely, they give the impression of a chance combination of manic depression and schizophrenia.

Strangely, this work was overlooked even by German authors such as Helmchen and Hippius (1967), who studied a large cohort of 120 schizophrenics who were having acute hospital treatment. Noting a substantial prevalence of depression in about half of their patients, they conceived the notion that this was caused by neuroleptic medication and coined the term *pharmacogenic depression* for this syndrome in schizophrenia.

Acute Studies

Knights and Hirsch were among several authors who challenged this concept when it was demonstrated that depressive symptoms in schizophrenia were most prevalent in the acute phase, just after admission to the hospital, and declined in intensity and frequency as the conditions stabilized (Knights and Hirsch 1981). They introduced the term *revealed depression* to draw attention to the fact that although

27

depressed symptoms are most prevalent in the acute phase of schizophrenia when patients are admitted to the hospital, they tend to go unnoticed or unappreciated because of florid psychotic symptoms. Their importance is later revealed to the clinician as the psychosis remits over the next 12 weeks because affective symptoms tended to persist. The patients were drawn from a total 1-year cohort of all patients seen within 2 weeks after admission to an acute psychiatric unit serving a catchment area of 90,000; patients who could cooperate with the interview were chosen. They also demonstrated that features of neurosis and depression in schizophrenia were almost as severe and prevalent 3 months after admission as symptoms of neurosis and depression in patients admitted with a neurotic or depressive diagnosis from the same 1-year cohort. This led to the hypothesis that affective symptoms are an inherent part of the disease process in schizophrenia, sharing with affective disorder common pathophysiological mechanisms. This observation was confirmed by Möller and Von Zerssen (1981) in a cohort of 280 acute patients, of whom 48% had depressive symptoms; by Johnson (1981) in a study of 30 acute admissions, 60% of whom had significant depressive symptoms; and by a reexamination of the International Pilot Study of Schizophrenia (World Health Organization 1973) of 588 patients in nine countries, of whom 80% had a depressive syndrome at the time of their acute illness. However, one problem with all these studies is that none report a substantial cohort of patients who are known to be drug-free at the time of admission, a problem addressed by Leff (Chapter 1, this volume.)

Follow-Up Studies

Studies that follow patients from the time they are discharged from the hospital (e.g., Johnson 1981; Knights et al. 1979) have found a lower point prevalence of schizophrenia, but the period prevalence is much higher. We found a point prevalence of 25% over 6 months, but our period prevalence was 53% over the same period (Knights et al. 1979). Johnson found that 70% of his cohort of chronic schizophrenic outpatients just recovered from an acute episode had had a significant depressive syndrome at one time or another over the 2-year follow-up period. These facts led us to hypothesize that affective symptoms are an integral part of the disease process of schizophrenia, sharing with affective disorder common pathophysiological mechanisms. This is a more modest concept than the suggestion that schizophrenia and affective disorders are actually the same disease (Wyatt et al. 1988).

Other Theories

Van Putten and May (1978) noted that there was a group of schizophrenic patients attending their clinic who had become extremely restless, irritable, and disturbed and gave the impression of having a depression. They originally called this "akinetic depression" because it responded immediately to an intravenous test dose of anticholinergic medication and therefore seemed to be a feature of drug-induced parkinsonism. On this point, hypotheses about the ideology of depression in schizophrenia can be divided into those that postulate that the affective features are apparent characteristics of schizophrenia itself (the illness-related hypothesis) and those that associate affective features with medication (the drug-related hypothesis). Because all prospective studies have shown that only a small percentage of patients (approximately less than 15%) have a schizophrenic episode after the acute illness without having equally severe depressive symptoms during the acute illness, we will not deal further with the concept of psychogenic "postpsychotic depression." Such depressions may be an understandable reaction of patients to their circumstances and the knowledge that they are ill, or these depressions may occur as a variation of the illness-related or drug-related problems, but appear after the acute illness. Depressive symptoms occur far too frequently in schizophrenia to be explained as a chance coincidence of manic depression and schizophrenia in the same patient.

NEW WORK

In the work we report here, we had set out to shed light on these issues by trying to replicate Johnson's (1981) placebo-controlled trial of the effect of anticholinergic drugs on depressive symptoms in schizophrenia, but chose to study chronic inpatients. Little attention had been paid to chronically hospitalized patients, but a study in this group raised new issues. Could the depressive symptoms of schizophrenia be artifacts of drug-induced parkinsonism because of reduced facial movements and reduced gestures (i.e., a misdiagnosis of parkinsonism as depression)? Or could the depressive symptoms be an artifact of the chronic negative syndrome of schizophrenia with poverty of affect, speech, content of speech, and movement (i.e., a misdiagnosis of the chronic negative features of schizophrenia)?

We studied a cohort of chronic schizophrenic patients at each of two large psychiatric hospitals. Because they were part of other ongoing studies, the sampling methods were not the same. At St. Bernards Hospital, the patients were identified by the nursing staff as possibly depressed and then referred to the research team for assessment, where they were given the Beck (Beck et al. 1961) and Hamilton (1960) rating scales. At Horton Hospital, 287 patients who had been diagnosed as having chronic schizophrenia were examined. Of 222 who met the DSM-III (American Psychiatric Association 1980) criteria for schizophrenia (Barnes et al., in press), 196 were able to be interviewed.

With these two cohorts we were able to test hypothesis I: *If depressive symptoms are an artifact of the negative symptoms of schizophrenia or of parkinsonian features, they should be more common in chronic schizophrenic patients in whom negative symptoms and parkinsonian symptoms can also be expected to be more common.* In fact, the point prevalence of depressive syndrome based on a Hamilton or Beck rating scale score of 15 or above among 46 patients tested at St. Bernards Hospital was only 7%. At Horton Hospital, 196 patients who met the DSM-III diagnosis of depression were rated by two psychiatrists on the Present State Examination (PSE) (Wing et al. 1974) item 23 for simple depression. Twenty-five patients with PSE-defined depressive mood were also assessed with the Montgomery-Asberg Depression Rating Scale (MADRS) (Montgomery and Asberg 1979). These 25 patients were matched for age, sex, and length of illness with a control group of otherwise similar nondepressed schizophrenic patients. The ratings for parkinsonism and akathisia were done independently and blind to the assessments of depression and negative symptoms. Only 13% of the Horton Hospital cohort had evidence of a depressed mood as defined by a rating of 2 or 3 on PSE item 23. This is a much lower prevalence of depression than we had expected in either sample. If we assume that there is a reasonably high level of negative symptoms and/or parkinsonian symptoms in these chronic hospitalized and neuroleptic- and other drug-medicated patients, the findings suggest that those with parkinsonism and/or negative symptoms are not being misdiagnosed as having depression to any great extent.

This leads us to hypothesis II: *If depression is an artifact of negative symptoms, or an artifact of parkinsonism, then we can also predict that chronic patients with depression would show negative symptoms or parkinsonism more often than a matched controlled group of chronic patients without depression.* This hypothesis was tested in the Horton Hospital cohort in 25 patients with depression and 25 nondepressed patients (Table 1).

Patients were tested with the MADRS, the Beck rating scale, and the affective flattening and alogia subscales of the Scale for the Assessment of Negative Symptoms (SANS) (Andreasen 1981). Patients were independently tested for parkinsonism using the clinical assessment of Mindham (1976) and the akathisia scale of Barnes and

Halstead (1988). We note that while patients with depression obviously have higher depression scores than the nondepressed group, there is no significant difference in the scores for affective flattening, alogia, parkinsonism, or akathisia. We can conclude from these data that PSE depression in chronic schizophrenic patients cannot be explained away (in this cohort) as an artifact of parkinsonism or negative symptoms in schizophrenia. (Note that the SANS and the Beck inventory were rated by a pair of investigators who were blind to the patient's PSE item 23 status and MADRS score for depression.)

Table 1. A Comparison of Institutionalized Patients with Chronic Schizophrenia, 25 with and 25 without Depression, Matched for Sex, Age, and Length of Illness at Horton Hospital

| | Present State Examination item 23 | | |
	With depression (score 1 or 2)	Without depression (score 0)	Rating scale
Mean ($\pm$ SD) scores			
Age	60.0 $\pm$ 13.0	61.0 $\pm$ 13.0	—
MADRS total**	15.9 $\pm$ 8.1	3.44 $\pm$ 4.6	MADRS
Beck total*	19.5 $\pm$ 10.9	10.2 $\pm$ 9.2	Beck
Affective flattening	11.4 $\pm$ 7.3	9.1 $\pm$ 5.7	SANS
Alogia	3.0 $\pm$ 2.2	1.96 $\pm$ 1.5	SANS
	n	%	*n*	%	
Parkinsonism					EPRS
no evidence	13	52	12	48	
discernable	7	28	7	28	
definitely present	3	12	5	20	
moderate/severe	2	8	1	4	
Akathisia	9	36	8	32	Barnes

Note. *p = .004; **p < .001. MADRS = Montgomery-Asberg Depression Rating Scale; SANS = Scale for the Assessment of Negative Symptoms; EPRS = Extrapyramidal Rating Scale.

The Relationship Between Depressive Symptoms and Extrapyramidal Symptoms in a Cohort of Mild Schizophrenic Outpatients

An ongoing study of stable schizophrenic outpatients at Charing Cross Hospital who did not have any positive symptoms but randomly were allocated to have active or placebo depot fluphenazine decanoate provided a possibility of testing two or more hypotheses: III. *If depressive symptoms are drug-related, they will be more common in patients who continue on antipsychotic medication than in patients who are withdrawn from drug treatment. IV. If depressive symptoms are an integral part of a schizophrenic syndrome, this may be reflected in the early stages of psychotic decompensation.* We will therefore look for an increase of a broad spectrum of neurotic and dysphoric symptoms as a first stage of schizophrenic decompensation.

The patients were engaged in a trial to test the efficacy of targeted early intermittently applied neuroleptic treatment as compared to continuous depot medication. Schizophrenic outpatients who were willing to go into the study were randomly allocated to continue depot medication or have placebo substituted. The 43 patients and their families were educated about schizophrenia and the need to contact the research team when dysphoric symptoms persisted 24 to 36 hours. If affective or dysphoric symptoms appeared, patients were given a 2-week supply of oral haloperidol, 10 mg daily. All the patients had a history of DSM-III positive schizophrenia with no florid symptoms in the previous 6 months. The study was carried out double-blind, and dysphoric symptoms were treated within 2 days of appearance. Patients who manifested psychotic symptoms for more than 8 weeks or on more than one occasion within 6 months were withdrawn from the trial as treatment failures, as were patients who refused to comply with the treatment program.

Patients were assessed with the Manchester Scale (Krawiecka et al. 1977) at 2-monthly intervals or whenever dysphoric symptoms were thought to be present if the Manchester depression score was 2 or higher. The 2-monthly assessments in each group were used to calculate the period prevalence of depression in the first and second 6-month periods of the study. Symptomatic episodes occurring between these 2-monthly assessments were not included in order to obtain an estimate of prevalence that is not based on equally regular assessments in both groups and not biased by the fact that if patients on placebo had (as they did) more dysphoric episodes occurring between 2-month ratings, they would be rated on these occasions when the control group would not.

Table 2 indicates the results of the Charing Cross cohort (Hirsch, Jolley, Barnes, unpublished observations) with respect to hypothesis III. There were no significant differences between the active and placebo depot treatment groups in the baseline prevalence of depression, in the period prevalence for depression during the first 6 months, or for the period prevalence of depression during the second 6 months. The period prevalence for depression was lower in the second 6 months than in the first 6 months in both groups, but these reductions were not significant. The lack of a significant difference between drug-treated and drug-withdrawn groups with respect to the prevalence of depression argues against depot neuroleptics (fluphenazine decanoate) being an important cause of depression in schizophrenia. Moreover, if one takes into account that spontaneous dysphoric episodes occurred in 76% of patients on placebo but in only 21% of patients on neuroleptics, then this provides evidence that neuroleptics prevent the reoccurrence of depressive and dysphoric symptoms in schizophrenic patients. This diminishes the importance of the fact that depot neuroleptics are detectable in the blood for 6 to 9 months after they have been withdrawn.

For the purpose of testing hypothesis IV, patients completed the SCL-90 (Derogatis 1977) monthly with the support of a psychiatric research worker, and again when a prodromal episode occurred, which triggered treatment, in which case the patient was reassessed 2 weeks later. We reasoned that if dysphoric symptoms are part of the acute schizophrenic syndrome, then they should appear more frequently in patients who are not receiving continuous neuroleptic

Table 2. Period Prevalence of Depression in Mild Chronic Outpatients: Intermittent versus Continuous Treatment Trial

Outpatients with a previous history of positive symptoms on:	N	First 6-month period prevalence		Second 6-month period prevalence	
		n	%	n	%
Active depot	22	4	18	3	14
Placebo depot	21	4	19	2	10

Note. Depression defined by Manchester Scale depression score ≥ 2. Patients were rated at 2-monthly intervals for depression, and the 6-month period prevalence was compared in patients on active medication and switched to placebo, and during the first and the second 6 months.

medication than in patients who have not had the medication withdrawn. However, we could not rule out the alternative interpretation that neuroleptic medication has a specific but separate effect in preventing recurrence of affective and dysphoric symptoms in patients with schizophrenia that is independent of acute schizophrenic symptomatology. Nor could we rule out the possibility that the appearance of dysphoric symptoms represents a rebound phenomenon that follows a discontinuation of neuroleptic medication or a lowering of the dose (analogous to withdrawal from narcotics). Using the SCL-90, we could also examine the question of whether depressive symptomatology is unique to the dysphoric syndrome or part of a much broader picture of neurotic and minor symptomatology representing a broad spectrum of reactivity that emerges prior to a schizophrenic relapse.

Table 3 shows the patients' individual SCL-90 subscores at three points in time for patients who had a dysphoric episode. The results show a significant increase in each of the SCL-90 subscores covering a broad range of symptomatology at the time that dysphoric symptoms are reported, as well as a significant increase in the average of the subscore (the Global Severity Index), including all patients who

Table 3. Mean SCL-90 Subscores for 22 Patients (6 Controls) Who Had a Dysphoric Episode, Recorded at Three Points in Time

	Mean item scores		
	Pre-onset (within 1 month)	Onset	Two weeks after onset
Somatization	0.413*	0.696	0.467
Depression	0.791**	1.223	0.745
Anxiety	0.514**	0.924	0.600
Phobic anxiety	0.374*	0.735	0.502
Obsessive-compulsive	0.593***	0.995	0.568
Psychoticism	0.505**	0.750	0.522
Paranoid	0.631**	0.992	0.585
Global Severity Index Interpersonal	0.812**	1.116	0.834

Note. Significant increase using Wilcoxon matched pairs test: $*p < .05$; $**p < .01$; $***p < .001$. Z for the Global Severity Index score was 3.4544.

had prodromal episodes. As referred to above, prodromal symptoms occurred in 76% of patients withdrawn from medication, compared with 27% of patients continuing on medication during 12 months of observation. (A recrudescence of specific schizophrenic symptomatology appeared in 33% of patients given placebo versus 7% of actively treated patients.) Nonpsychotic prodromal symptoms preceded 73% of psychotic episodes. In most cases, the prodromal episodes remitted within 2 weeks of starting haloperidol, although this improvement could simply reflect the natural history of such episodes. These results provide tentative support for hypothesis IV and are consistent with the Foulds and Bedford (1975) concept of a hierarchy of psychiatric symptoms in the emergence of psychiatric phenomena, as discussed by Leff (Chapter 1, this volume).

CONCLUSION

Different ongoing studies in our department have provided an opportunity to examine a number of hypotheses about the nature of depressive and dysphoric symptoms that occur in patients with diagnosed schizophrenia. We were surprised to find a low prevalence of depression in chronic schizophrenic inpatients in two psychiatric hospitals. Failure to diagnose depression in such chronic patients who are characterized by negative symptoms and long-standing illness could be related to their difficulty in expressing their feelings or to their lack of interest in completing self-rating scales. However, the Horton Hospital sample, which compared chronic patients with depressive symptoms to a control group of chronic patients, demonstrated that chronic patients are able to fill out self-rating scales and that the depressive symptoms are not related to parkinsonian side effects.

Consistent with the literature (e.g., Hirsch 1982), we have again found that depressive symptoms are no more prevalent among patients who have been withdrawn from medication than among patients who continue on active depot medication as determined by regular 2-monthly assessments over a 12-month period. However, this does not take into account the frequency of spontaneous dysphoric symptoms, which are three times as prevalent in the patients on placebo medication as in patients on active medication. These findings disconfirm the concept that depressive or dysphoric symptoms are more common in patients who are on depot neuroleptic medication. Our results support the view that depressive and dysphoric symptoms are not frequently due to the parkinsonian effects of neuroleptics, akathisia, and akinesia. On the other hand, depressive symptoms are but part of a broad range of nonspecific dysphoric symptoms in schizophrenia, which we have shown occur more frequently in patients who are withdrawn from depot medication than in patients who continue on the medication.

Our results suggest that depressive and dysphoric symptoms do not represent misidentification of the negative symptoms of schizophrenia, affective flattening, and alogia, as measured by the SANS. On the other hand, previous results suggest that affective symptoms are most prevalent in the acute phase of schizophrenia, and that they come and go spontaneously, which may represent a potential reactivation of the schizophrenic syndrome.

REFERENCES

American Psychiatric Association: Diagnostic and Statistical Manual of Mental Disorders, Third Edition. Washington, DC, American Psychiatric Association, 1980

Andreasen NC: Scale for the Assessment of Negative Symptoms (SANS). Iowa City, University of Iowa, 1981

Barnes TRE, Halstead SM: A scale for rating drug-induced akathisia (abstract). Schizophrenia Research 1:249, 1988

Barnes TRE, Curson DA, Liddle PF, et al: The nature and prevalence of depression in chronic schizophrenic inpatients. Br J Psychiatry 154:486–491, 1989

Beck AT, Ward CH, Mendelsohn I, et al: An inventory for measuring depression. Arch Gen Psychiatry 4:561–571, 1961

Bleuler M: Die Prognose der Dementia Praecox (Schizophreniegroppe). Allgemeine Zeitschrift vol 65, 1908

Derogatis LR: SCL-90: administration, scoring and procedures manual for the revised version. Baltimore, Clinical Psychometrics Research Unit, 1977

Foulds GA, Bedford A: Hierarchy of classes of personal illness. Psychol Med 5:181–192, 1975

Hamilton M: A rating scale used for depression. J Neurol Neurosurg Psychiatry 23:56–62, 1960

Helmchen H, Hippius H: Depressive Syndrome im Verlauf neuronleptischer Therapie. Nervenarzt 38:445, 1967

Hirsch SR: Revealed depression in schizophrenia. Br J Psychiatry 139:89–101, 1982

Hirsch SR, Gaind R, Rohde PD, et al: Outpatient maintenance of chronic schizophrenic patients with long-acting fluphenazine: double-blind placebo trial. Br Med J 192:633–637, 1973

Johnson DAW: Studies of depressive symptoms in schizophrenia. Br J Psychiatry 139:89–101, 1981

Knights A, Hirsch SR: Revealed depression and drug treatment for schizophrenia. Arch Gen Psychiatry 38:806–811, 1981

Knights A, Okasha MS, Salih M, et al: Depressive and extrapyramidal symptoms and clinical effects: a trial of fluphenazine versus flupenthixol in maintenance of schizophrenic outpatients. Br J Psychiatry 135:515–523, 1979

Krawiecka M, Goldberg D, Vaughan M: A standardised psychiatric assessment scale for rating chronic psychotic patients. Acta Psychiatr Scand 55:299–308, 1977

Mindham RHS: Assessment of drug-induced extrapyramidal reactions and of drugs given for their control. Br J Clin Pharmacol 3 (suppl 2):395–400, 1976

Möller HJ, Von Zerssen D: Depressive Symptomatik in stationaren Behandlungsverlauf von 280 schizophrenen patienten. Pharmacopsychiatrica 14:172–179, 1981

Montgomery SA, Asberg M: A new depression scale designed to be sensitive to change. Br J Psychiatry 134:382–389, 1979

Van Putten T, May PRA: Akinetic depression in schizophrenia. Arch Gen Psychiatry 35:1101–1107, 1978

Wing JK, Cooper JE, Sartorius N: The measurement and classification of psychiatric symptoms. New York, Cambridge University Press, 1974

World Health Organization: The International Pilot Study of Schizophrenia, Vol. 1. Geneva, World Health Organization, 1973

Wyatt RJ, Alexander RC, Egan MF, et al: Schizophrenia, just the facts, what do we know and how well do we know it? Schizophrenia Research 1:3–18, 1988

Chapter 3

Relationship Between Depression and Suicidal Behavior in Schizophrenia

Alec Roy, M.B.

Chapter 3

Relationship Between Depression and Suicidal Behavior in Schizophrenia

Bleuler (1950) described the suicidal drive as "the most serious of schizophrenic symptoms" (p. 488). More recent studies suggest that depression is common during the course of schizophrenic illness (Roy 1980, 1981). The purpose of this chapter is to examine whether or not there is a relationship between depression and suicidal behavior in schizophrenia. Depression in relation to both completed and attempted suicide will be considered.

SUICIDE

Incidence

Numerous follow-up studies of schizophrenic patients over the last 45 years have reported that schizophrenic illness carries with it an increased risk of suicide. In 1977, Miles reviewed all the then-published follow-up studies and concluded that up to 10% of schizophrenic patients die by suicide. He estimated that, at that time in the United States, there were approximately 3,800 schizophrenic patients who committed suicide each year.

There are large variations between studies for the calculated suicide risk for schizophrenic patients. In 1964, using the records of the Houston Veterans Administration Hospital, Pokorny calculated that the annual suicide rate for male schizophrenic patients was 167/100,000 compared with the then United States national rate of about 10/100,000. More recently, from the Missouri Psychiatry Case Register, Evenson et al. (1982) estimated that the age-adjusted annual suicide rate for male schizophrenic patients was 210/100,000; the rate for females was lower at 90/100,000. Also in 1982, using the Camberwell Psychiatric Case Register, Wilkinson estimated that the

41

annual suicide rate for first-admission schizophrenic patients was between 500 and 750/100,000. In reported series of psychiatric patients known to have committed suicide, schizophrenic patients usually account for up to a third of such patients (Roy 1982a, 1985, 1986a, 1986b).

Clinical Correlates

Schizophrenic patients who commit suicide tend to be male and young. The first few years of schizophrenic illness are a period of increased risk for suicide. Schizophrenic patients tend to commit suicide in relationship to their last psychiatric hospitalization. Approximately 30% of schizophrenic patient suicide victims commit suicide while they are inpatients, although not usually in the hospital itself. Among schizophrenic outpatients, the first few weeks and months after discharge from a hospitalization are a period of increased suicide risk (reviewed in Roy 1986a, 1986b).

Depression

Studies reported over the last 30 years strongly suggest that depression is closely associated with suicide in schizophrenic patients. Depressive symptoms have been noted in the last period of psychiatric contact in a substantial percentage of schizophrenic patient suicide victims. There have been nine studies reporting on the presence or absence of associated affective symptoms. Among the total of 270 schizophrenic patient suicide victims in these studies, affective symptoms were noted during the period of contact before the patient committed suicide in approximately 60% (Table 1). Similarly, in a 10th study, Beisser and Blanchette (1961) reported a "high frequency of depression" among 32 schizophrenic patient suicide victims.

Nature of Depressive Symptoms

There has been some recent discussion about the type of depressive symptoms that are found among schizophrenic suicide victims. Early uncontrolled studies (e.g., Yarden 1974) reported severe affective symptoms in the period antedating suicide. For example, 80% of his suicide victims had anorexia and weight loss, 65% hopelessness and despair, and 45% motor disturbance (Table 2).

In a more recent controlled study, Roy (1982b) compared 30 chronic schizophrenic suicide victims with 30 living chronic schizophrenic control patients matched for age and sex. Significantly more of the suicides than the controls had in the past both been diagnosed as suffering from an associated depressive episode and treated for depression with either antidepressants or electroconvulsive therapy

(ECT) (Table 3). Of the 30 suicides, 17 (56.6%) had had a past depressive episode, and 14 (46.6%) had been treated with antidepressants or ECT for depression. Similarly, in their last period of psychiatric contact, 16 (53.3%) of the 30 suicides were diagnosed

Table 1.   Clinical Studies Reporting Absence or Presence of Depression in Last Period of Contact Among Chronic Schizophrenic Patient Suicide Victims

Reference	Suicide victims N	Suicide victims with depression	
		n	%
Levy and Southcombe (1953)	23	6	25.2
Cohen et al. (1964)	40	28	70
Warnes (1968)	16	12	75
Yarden (1974)	20	13	65
Virkkunen (1974)	82	57	69.5
Cheng (1982)	12	12	100
Roy (1982b)	30	16	53.3
Drake et al. (1984)	15	12	80
Allebeck et al. (1987)	32	4	12.5
TOTAL	270	160	59.3

Table 2.   Affective Symptoms Before Suicide Among 20 Schizophrenic Patient Suicide Victims

Affective symptoms	N	%
Anorexia and weight loss	16	80
Motor disturbances		
Restlessness	9	45
Retardation	9	45
Expressions of hopelessness and despair	13	65
Direct verbal statements of suicidal intent	10	50
Delusions of guilt or wrongdoing or of morbid content; hallucinations prompting to suicide or having an accusatory, condemning nature	9	45
Aggressive outbursts	7	35

Note. From Yarden (1974), published with permission from Comprehensive Psychiatry.

as suffering from a depressive episode compared with only 4 (13.3%) controls (Table 3).

Further interesting findings in relationship to depression were noted when the suicide victims and controls were compared for the reasons for all their admissions to the postgraduate psychiatric hospital where they received most of their treatment. Significantly more of the admissions of the eventual suicide victims were for a mental state consisting of a mixture of schizophrenic and affective symptoms (Table 4). On the contrary, significantly more of the admissions of the living controls were for a mental state consisting of schizophrenic symptoms alone.

Similar results were obtained when the reason for the last psychiatric hospital admission was examined. Significantly more of the eventual suicide victims had their last admission because of associated suicidal impulses or depressive symptoms (Table 5). It is of note that the majority of these patients committed suicide in relationship to their last admission—either during it (the minority) or in the weeks or months after discharge from it.

Drake and Cotton (1986) have examined further the relationship

Table 3. Schizophrenic Patient Suicide Victims and Living Schizophrenic Patient Controls Compared for History of Depression

	Schizophrenic suicides (N = 30)	Age- and sex-matched schizophrenic controls (N = 30)	Significance
Psychiatric history			
Psychiatric disorder in first-degree relatives	8	5	NS
Past depressive episode	17	5	.001
Past treatment for depression	14	7	.05
Previous suicide attempt	12	11	NS
Last episode			
Depressed in last episode	16	4	.001
Treated for depression in last episode	9	6	NS

Note. From Roy 1982b, published with permission from British Journal of Psychiatry.

Table 4. Schizophrenic Patient Suicide Victims and Controls Compared for the Reason for All Their Psychiatric Admissions to the Clarke Institute of Psychiatry in Toronto

	Schizophrenic suicides (N = 27)		Age- and sex-matched schizophrenic controls (N = 25)		Significance
	n	%	*n*	%	
1. Schizophrenic symptoms plus depressive episode	15	17.4	4	6.7	.05
2. Schizophrenic symptoms plus suicide	18	20.9	7	11.7	NS
3. Depressive episode	1	1.2	1	1.7	NS
4. Situational crisis	7	8.1	1	1.7	NS
5. Schizophrenic symptoms only	45	52.3	47	78.3	.01

Note. From Roy (1982b), published with permission from British Journal of Psychiatry.

Table 5. Schizophrenic Patient Suicide Victims and Controls Compared for Reason for Last Psychiatric Hospital Admission

	Schizophrenic suicides (N = 29)	Age- and sex-matched schizophrenic controls (N = 28)	Significance
1. Schizophrenic symptoms plus depressive episode	7	2	NS
2. Schizophrenic symptoms plus suicidal	8	3	NS
3. Depressive episode	1	2	NS
4. 1, 2, and 3 together	16	7	.02
5. Situational crisis	3	2	NS
6. Schizophrenic symptoms only	10	19	.01

Note. From Roy (1982b), published with permission from British Journal of Psychiatry.

between depression and suicide. They compared 15 schizophrenic suicide victims with 89 schizophrenic patients who did not commit suicide. Two research assistants, blind to the outcome, independently rated the hospital records for features of depression according to DSM-III (American Psychiatric Association 1980) criteria. The research assistants also rated hopelessness according to statements similar to those found in the hopelessness scale of the Beck Depression Inventory (Beck et al. 1961).

The comparison of schizophrenic suicide victims and controls showed that the suicides were much more likely to manifest persistent depressed mood as well as many of the other features of depression during their index hospital admission. They were not, however, significantly more likely to meet the criteria for a major depressive episode. Breaking down the depressive symptoms into somatic and psychological symptoms revealed the reason for this. The suicides clearly demonstrated the psychological features of depression, including hopelessness, but not the somatic symptoms that are needed to make the diagnosis of a major depressive episode (Table 6).

In this interesting study, Drake and Cotton (1986) went on to

Table 6. Schizophrenic Suicide Victims and Nonsuicides Compared for Depressive Symptoms

Variable	Suicides (N = 15)	Nonsuicides (N = 89)	Significance
Severity of depression			
Persistent depressed mood (at least 2 weeks)	80	48	.01
Major depressive episode (DSM-III)	33	19	NS
Somatic symptoms			
Appetite or weight disturbance	20	24	NS
Sleep disturbance	40	31	NS
Psychomotor disturbance	80	51	.05
Loss of energy	20	8	NS
Psychological symptoms			
Worthlessness, self-reproach, or guilt	53	23	.01
Suicide ideas	87	44	.01
Hopelessness	67	20	.01

Note. From Drake and Cotton (1986), published with permission from British Journal of Psychiatry.

examine the relative contribution of depression and hopelessness to suicide. Although the presence of persistent depressed mood increased the risk of suicide, severity of depression, as measured by a major depressive episode, did not further increase the risk of suicide. On the other hand, the development of hopelessness in addition to a depressed mood significantly augmented the probability of suicide. Furthermore, in the absence of hopelessness, depressed schizophrenic patients were at no greater statistical risk for suicide than nondepressed schizophrenic patients (Table 7).

Drake and Cotton (1986) noted that their schizophrenic suicide victims had shown high premorbid achievement, high self-expectations of performance, and high awareness of their pathology (Cotton et al. 1985; Drake et al. 1984). For example, 73% of the suicide victims were college educated compared with 29% of the controls. Drake and Cotton made the important point that, in such patients:

> Given their inability to achieve major life goals, they felt inadequate, feared further deterioration of their mental abilities, and decided to end their lives rather than continue living with chronic mental illness. To the extent that their decisions represented realistic estimations of current and future functioning in relation to goals, rather than mood-distorted perceptions of the future, perhaps these patients should be considered to suffer from despair rather than depression . . . . [they] are likely to experience hopelessness defined as negative expectancies about the future and other psychological features of depression.

Risk Factors for Suicide

Studies have suggested the likely risk factors for suicide in schizophrenic patients. These include being young and male, having a

Table 7. Depression, Hopelessness, and Probability of Suicide

	Total N	Suicide n	Probability of suicide
Entire sample	104	15	0.14
Patients with depressed mood	56	12	0.22
with major depressive episode	22	5	0.23
with hopelessness	27	10	0.37
without hopelessness	29	2	0.07
Patients without depressed mood	48	3	0.06

Note. From Drake and Cotton (1986), reproduced with permission from British Journal of Psychiatry.

relapsing illness, having been depressed in the past, being currently depressed, having been admitted in the last period of psychiatric contact with accompanying depressive symptoms or suicidal ideas, having changed recently from inpatient to outpatient care, and being socially isolated in the community (Roy 1982a, 1982b; reviewed in Drake et al. 1985).

Drake et al. (1984) set out to determine which of these risk factors distinguished 15 schizophrenic patient suicides from 89 living schizophrenic patients. They, too, found that the suicides were young; the majority were male and had a chronic illness with numerous exacerbations and remissions (a mean 6.8 admissions during a mean 8.4 years of illness). At their last hospitalization, significantly more of them were depressed (80%), felt inadequate (80%), felt hopeless (60%), and had suicidal ideation (73%) (Table 8). Of the outpatient suicides in the study, 70% killed themselves within 6 months of discharge. Significantly more of the suicides lived alone (60%).

Prediction of Suicide

These risk factors may well be useful in the acute short-term suicide risk assessment of schizophrenic patients. However, unfortunately, they are probably of limited value in the long-range prediction of eventual suicide. Shaffer et al. (1974) carried out a 5-year follow-up study of 361 schizophrenic patients admitted to the Phipps Clinic at Johns Hopkins Hospital. They found that 12 of these patients

Table 8. Comparison of Schizophrenic Patients Who Did and Did Not Commit Suicide, in Percentages

	Suicides (N = 15)	Nonsuicides (N = 89)	Significance
College education	73	29	.01
Explicit suicide threat	67	28	.01
Lives alone	60	27	.01
Depressed mood	80	48	.01
Inadequate	80	36	.01
Hopeless	60	27	.01
Suicidal ideation	73	38	.01
Awareness of pathology	47	11	.01
Fears of mental disintegration	33	1	.01
High self-expectations	47	12	.01

Note. From Drake et al. (1984), published with permission from Journal of Nervous and Mental Diseases.

eventually commited suicide. However, none of the signs and ratings derived from the case notes of the index admission, either singly or in combinations, accurately predicted the 12 patients known to have committed suicide.

Similarly, we recently carried out a follow-up study of 100 chronic schizophrenic inpatients seen at the National Institute of Mental Health (NIMH) (Roy et al. 1986). This revealed that 6 of the 100 patients had committed suicide over the mean 4.5 years of the follow-up period. We used seven combinations of socio-demographic and clinical variables, recorded at their index NIMH admission, to try to identify these six suicide victims (Table 9). Having had a major depressive episode was one of the variables used. Five of the seven "strategies" used identified only one of the six patients who eventually committed suicide; one strategy identified none, and another identified only two of the six suicide victims.

In our study (Roy et al. 1986), all the other patients identified by the seven strategies fell within the group of 94 patients known not to have committed suicide. In fact, five of the seven strategies iden-

Table 9. Seven Combinations of Clinical Features, Determined at the Index Admission, Used as "Strategies" to Try to Identify the 6 Schizophrenic Patients Determined at Follow-Up to Have Committed Suicide

Category of patient at index admission	Number of patients identified in each category	Number of patients who subsequently committed suicide
1. Onset under 25 years, past depression, 5 + admissions	10	1
2. Onset under 25 years, past depression, 7 + admissions	5	1
3. Onset under 25 years, past depression, total length of admissions total over a year, 2 or more past suicide attempts	4	1
4. 2 or more past suicide attempts	15	2
5. 3 or more past suicide attempts	6	1
6. 4 or more past suicide attempts	2	1
7. 5 or more past suicide attempts	1	0

Note. An individual suicide victim could be identified in one or more category. From Roy et al. (1986), published with permission from Canadian Journal of Psychiatry.

tified from 3 to 12 patients as at risk for committing suicide who were still alive. Four of the six patients who did commit suicide were not identified by any of the seven strategies used.

The difficulty of the long-term prediction of suicide is well recognized. This was recently demonstrated in a large study of psychiatric patients by Pokorny (1983). Twenty-one items were used to identify, among a consecutive series of 4,800 admissions, a subsample of 803 patients who were thought to be at high risk for suicide. A 5-year follow-up study revealed that 67 of the patients had subsequently committed suicide. Of these 67, 37 were not found among the high-risk subsample (false negatives), whereas 766 of the 803 patients thought to have a high risk for suicide were, in fact, alive (false positives).

In the studies of Shaffer et al. (1974) and Roy et al. (1986), the inability to identify the majority of the schizophrenic patients who subsequently committed suicide supports Pokorny's (1983) conclusion that it "is inescapable that we do not possess any item of information or any combination of items that permits us to identify to a useful degree the particular persons who will commit suicide." However, the work of Drake and Cotton (1986) has suggested that the depressive symptom of hopelessness is particularly closely associated with schizophrenic suicide victims. The predictive power of this important symptom, either alone or in combination with other variables, has not as yet been further investigated.

ATTEMPTED SUICIDE

Incidence

Unfortunately, there is little information about how many schizophrenic patients attempt suicide. What data there are come from a variety of different studies. Some studies report the incidence of suicide attempts among newly admitted schizophrenic patients. Others report the incidence over the whole course of illness among long-term institutionalized patients. Still others report the incidence among schizophrenic outpatients over varying follow-up periods after discharge from an index hospitalization. However, taken together, these various sources of evidence reveal that a substantial percentage of schizophrenic patients do attempt suicide at some time during the course of their illness. The reported percentages vary from 18% to 55.1%, depending on the nature of the study (reviewed in Roy 1986a, 1986b). The mean is about 30%.

Suicidal ideation is also common among schizophrenic patients. For example, McGlashan (1984) followed up 163 chronic schizophrenic patients discharged from Chestnut Lodge Hospital, Maryland, between 1950 and 1975. He found that, over a mean of 15 years of follow-up, not only had 24% of the schizophrenic patients attempted suicide, but 40% of them had had suicidal thoughts.

Depressive Symptoms and Suicide Attempts

There have been six studies examining for an association between depressive symptoms and attempts at suicide among schizophrenic patients. Roy et al. (1984) found that significantly more of the 70 schizophrenic patients who at some time had made a suicide attempt, when compared with the 57 patients who had never attempted suicide, had a lifetime history of a major depressive episode and had at some time been treated with antidepressant medication (Table 10).

Another recent study (Celeste Johns, personal communication, 1985) found that 23 (37.1%) of 62 schizophrenic patients who had attempted suicide at some time rated themselves as significantly more depressed at the index hospitalization than did the 39 patients who had not attempted suicide; they also had significantly higher Hamilton (1960) depression scores (28 versus 21, $p < .01$).

Prasad and colleagues have used the Present State Examination (PSE) in two studies examining whether there are symptomatic differences between schizophrenic patients who do or do not attempt suicide. In the first small study (Prasad 1986), 55 hospitalized schizophrenic patients were interviewed and their case notes examined

Table 10.   Schizophrenic Patients Who Had or Had Not Attempted Suicide Compared for Whether or Not They Had a Depressive Episode or Treatment for Depression

	Attempted suicide (N = 70)	Never attempted suicide (N = 57)	Significance
Had a major depressive episode	32	6	.001
Treated with antidepressant medications at some time	46	24	.01
Received a course of electroconvulsive therapy	18	4	.01

Note. From Roy et al. (1984), published with permission from British Journal of Psychiatry.

to determine how many of them had attempted suicide in the previous year. Significantly more of the 25 patients who had attempted suicide were rated as having various affective symptoms on the PSE when compared with the 30 patients who had not attempted suicide (Table 11).

Prasad and Kumar (1988) enlarged this initial small series of patients. Again, significantly more of the 131 schizophrenic patients who had attempted suicide were rated as having various affective symptoms on the PSE when compared with the 70 patients who had not attempted suicide (Table 12).

In a second study, to escape the potentially confounding variable of a hospital admission, Prasad and Kellner (1988) examined 417 schizophrenic day patients. Again, significantly greater percentages of the 193 patients who had attempted suicide were rated as having various affective symptoms on the PSE than the 224 patients who had never attempted suicide (Table 13).

In another study, Drake et al. (1986) compared 15 schizophrenic suicide victims with 19 schizophrenic patients who had made a suicide attempt (Table 14). Both groups had associated affective symptoms. However, the comparison showed that significantly more of the suicide completers than attempters had depressed mood and felt inadequate, hopeless, and worthless. Significantly more of the suicide victims had lived alone while significantly more of the suicide at-

Table 11. Schizophrenic Inpatients Who Had or Had Not Attempted Suicide Compared for Affective Symptoms

Symptoms	Attempted suicide ($N = 25$)	No suicide attempt ($N = 30$)	Significance
Pathological guilt	13	7	.05
Nervous tension	22	10	.01
Tiredness	20	11	.01
Self-depreciation	24	5	.01
Subjective anergia and retardation	12	3	.05
Lack of self-confidence	22	6	.01
Depressed mood	25	7	.01
Hopelessness	18	5	.01
Neglect due to brooding	21	11	.05
Suicidal plans or acts	22	10	.05

Note. From Prasad (1986), published with permission from Acta Psychiatrica Scandinavica.

Table 12.   Significant Differences for Affective Symptoms Between Schizophrenic Inpatients Who Had or Had Not Attempted Suicide

Symptoms	Attempted suicide (N = 131)		No suicide attempt (N = 70)	
	n	%	n	%
Pathological guilt	78	59.5	15	21.4
Nervous tension	96	73.3	24	34.3
Tiredness	75	57.2	17	24.3
Self-depreciation	110	84.0	10	14.3
Lack of self-confidence	111	84.7	34	48.6
Depressed mood	117	89.3	24	34.3
Hopelessness	89	67.9	24	34.3
Neglect due to brooding	91	69.5	34	48.6
Suicidal plans or acts	68	51.9	15	21.4
Morning depression	44	33.6	16	22.9

Note. From Prasad and Kumar (1988), published with permission from Guilford Press.

Table 13.   Significant Differences for Affective Symptoms Between Schizophrenic Day Patients Who Had or Had Not Attempted Suicide

Symptoms	Attempted suicide (N = 193)		Never attempted suicide (N = 224)		Significance
	n	%	n	%	
Pathological guilt	50	25.9	8	3.6	.02
Nervous tension	63	32.6	24	10.7	.02
Tiredness	53	27.5	11	4.9	.01
Self-depreciation	51	26.4	31	13.8	.05
Subjective anergic and retardation	38	19.7	9	4.0	.02
Lack of self-confidence	52	26.9	23	10.3	.02
Depressed mood	51	26.4	24	10.7	.05
Neglect due to brooding	37	19.2	11	4.9	.05

Note. From Prasad and Kellner (1988), published with permission from Acta Psychiatrica Scandinavica.

tempters lived with families or others. This interesting study suggests that schizophrenic patients who commit suicide are more depressed, suicidal, and socially isolated than those who attempt suicide.

Thus all six studies examining for an association between depressive symptoms and suicide attempts among schizophrenic patients have reported a positive relationship. These findings are in accord with recent studies of suicide attempters in the general population. These studies have reported that between 35% and 79% of suicide attempters have associated depressive symptoms (reviewed in Roy 1986a).

Studies of depressed schizophrenics also reveal an association with suicidal behavior. For example, we compared 18 depressed schizophrenic outpatients with 18 nondepressed schizophrenic outpatients (Roy et al. 1983). All the patients were well controlled on neuroleptics. As might have been expected, significantly more of the depressed schizophrenic patients had attempted suicide at some time. Also, significantly more of the depressed schizophrenic patients lived alone, had low self-esteem, had early parental loss, and had had more

Table 14. A Comparison of Schizophrenic Patients Who Completed Suicide with Schizophrenic Patients Who Attempted Suicide

Characteristics	Suicides (N = 15)	Controls (N = 19)	Significance
Age (years)	31.7	24.8	NS
Sex (male)	60%	47%	NS
Previous suicide attempt	73%	47%	NS
Three or more attempts	40%	21%	NS
Explicit suicide threat	67%	16%	.01
Lives with family of origin	27%	63%	.05
Lives alone	60%	11%	.01
Depressed mood	80%	52%	.05
Feels inadequate	80%	42%	.05
Hopelessness	67%	26%	.05
Worthlessness	53%	21%	.05
Suicidal ideation	87%	37%	.01
Fears of mental disintegration	33%	5%	.05
High self-expectations	47%	16%	.06
Improved at discharge	67%	32%	.05

Note. From Drake et al. (1986), published with permission from British Journal of Psychiatry.

life events in the 6 months before the onset of depression (Table 15). Thus it may be that depressive symptoms (and suicidal behavior) in schizophrenic outpatients, well controlled by neuroleptics, may occur in those who also have risk factors for depression and who experience an excess of life events (Roy 1983).

CONCLUSION

Suicidal behavior is usually multidetermined. However, it seems clear that in some schizophrenic patients there is an association between depressive symptoms and both completed and attempted suicide. Suicidal behavior among schizophrenic patients occurs mainly among outpatients. This suggests the need for prospective studies of cohorts of schizophrenic outpatients. Such studies might look more closely at predisposing and precipitating factors in the etiology of depression and suicidal behavior among schizophrenic patients.

Table 15. Significant Differences Between Depressed and Nondepressed Schizophrenic Outpatients

	Depressed schizophrenics ($N = 18$)	Nondepressed schizophrenics ($N = 18$)	Significance
Number of admissions	6.9	4.1	.02
Past depressive episode	15	5	.001
Past treatment for depression	13	5	.009
Previous suicide attempt	15	7	.007
Early parental loss	11	5	.05
Low self-esteem	20.9	29.7	.005
Living alone	11	4	.02
Number of life events in previous 6 months	4.0	1.4	.0005

Note. From Roy et al. (1983), published with permission from British Journal of Psychiatry.

REFERENCES

Allebeck P, Varla E, Kristjansson E, et al: Risk factors for suicide among patients with schizophrenia. Acta Psychiatr Scand 76:414–419, 1987

American Psychiatric Association: Diagnostic and Statistical Manual of Mental Disorders, Third Edition. Washington, DC, American Psychiatric Association, 1980

Beck AT, Ward CH, Mendelsohn I, et al: An inventory for measuring depression. Arch Gen Psychiatry 4:561–571, 1961

Beisser A, Blanchette J: A study of suicides in a mental hospital. Journal of Diseases of the Nervous System 22:365–369, 1961

Bleuler E: Demential Praecox or the Group of Schizophrenias. New York, International Universities Press, 1950

Cheng L: Suicide in schizophrenia. Paper presented at the annual meeting of The Royal College of Physicians and Surgeons. Toronto, Canada, 1982

Cohen S, Leonard C, Farberow N, et al: Tranquilizers and suicide in the schizophrenic patients. Arch Gen Psychiatry 11:312–321, 1964

Cotton P, Drake R, Gates C: Critical treatment issues in suicide among schizophrenics. Hosp Community Psychiatry 36:534–536, 1985

Drake R, Cotton P: Depression, hopelessness, and suicide in chronic schizophrenia. Br J Psychiatry 148:554–559, 1986

Drake R, Gates C, Cotton P, et al: Suicide among schizophrenics: who is at risk? J Nerv Ment Dis 172:613–617, 1984

Drake R, Gates C, Whitaker A, et al: Suicide among schizophrenics: a review. Compr Psychiatry 26:90–100, 1985

Drake R, Gates C, Cotton P: Suicide among schizophrenics: a comparison of attempters and completed suicides. Br J Psychiatry 149:784–787, 1986

Evenson R, Wood J, Nuttall E, al al: Suicide rates among public mental health patients. Acta Psychiatr Scand 66:254–264, 1982

Hamilton M: A rating scale for depression. J Neurol Neurosurg Psychiatry 23:56–62, 1960

Levy S, Southcombe R: Suicide in a state hospital for the mentally ill. J Nerv Ment Dis 117:504–514, 1953

McGlashan T: The Chestnut Lodge follow-up study: part II, long-term outcome of schizophrenia and the affective disorders. Arch Gen Psychiatry 41:586–601, 1984

Miles P: Conditions predisposing to suicide: a review. J Nerv Ment Dis 164:231–246, 1977

Pokorny A: Suicide rates in various psychiatric disorders. J Nerv Ment Dis 139:499–506, 1964

Pokorny A: Prediction of suicide in psychiatric patients. Arch Gen Psychiatry 40:249–257, 1983

Prasad A: Attempted suicide in hospitalized schizophrenics. Acta Psychiatr Scand 74:41–42, 1986

Prasad A, Kellner P: Suicidal behaviour in schizophrenic day patients. Acta Psychiatr Scand 77:488–490, 1988

Prasad A, Kumar N: Suicidal behavior in hospitalized schizophrenics. Suicide Life Threat Behav 18:265–269, 1988

Roy A: Depression in chronic paranoid schizophrenia. Br J Psychiatry 137:138–139, 1980

Roy A: Depression in the course of chronic undifferentiated schizophrenia. Arch Gen Psychiatry 38:296–300, 1981

Roy A: Risk factors for suicide in psychiatric patients. Arch Gen Psychiatry 39:1089–1095, 1982a

Roy A: Suicide in chronic schizophrenia. Br J Psychiatry 141:171–177, 1982b

Roy A: Depression in chronic schizophrenia, in Psychiatry: The State of the Art, Vol 1. Edited by Pichot P, Berner P, Wolf R, et al. New York, Plenum, 1983, pp 609–611

Roy A: Suicide and psychiatric patients. Psychiatr Clin North Am 8:227–241, 1985

Roy A: Depression and suicide in chronic schizophrenia. Psychiatr Clin North Am 9:193–206, 1986a

Roy A: Suicide in schizophrenia, in Suicide. Edited by Roy A. Baltimore, Williams & Wilkins, 1986b

Roy A, Thompson R, Kennedy S: Depression in chronic schizophrenia. Br J Psychiatry 142:465–470, 1983

Roy A, Mazonson A, Pickar D: Attempted suicide in chronic schizophrenia. Br J Psychiatry 144:303–306, 1984

Roy A, Schreiber J, Mazonson A, et al: Suicidal behavior in chronic schizophrenic patients: a follow-up study. Can J Psychiatry 31:737–740, 1986

Shaffer J, Perlin S, Schmidt C, et al: The prediction of suicide in schizophrenia. J Nerv Ment Dis 159:349–355, 1974

Virkkunen M: Suicide in schizophrenia and paranoid psychosis. Acta Psychiatr Scand [Suppl] 250:1–305, 1974

Warnes H: Suicide in schizophrenia. Diseases of the Nervous System 29:35–40, 1968

Wilkinson D: The suicide rate in schizophrenia. Br J Psychiatry 140:138–141, 1982

Yarden P: Observations on suicide in chronic schizophrenics. Compr Psychiatry 15:325–333, 1974

Chapter 4

Diagnostic Separateness of Schizophrenia and Affective Disorder

Keith L. Rogers, M.D.
George Winokur, M.D.

Chapter 4

Diagnostic Separateness of Schizophrenia and Affective Disorder

Prior to the writings of Kraepelin at the beginning of this century, clinicians thought of mental illness as a continuum. In other words, it was believed that illnesses blended imperceptibly one into another. A continuum of severity is frequently implied. Kraepelin observed many patients directly and formulated the original clinical distinction between affective disorder (manic-depressive illness) and schizophrenia (dementia praecox) based on age and type of onset, clinical symptoms, and course of illness. By and large, this basic distinction has survived intact to this day, to the point where the concept is taken for granted as being "true." But is the differentiation as clear as the original description implied? It is well-known that there are a great many patients that fit the dichotomy quite nicely, following an episodic versus a chronic course, having full recovery versus eventual deterioration, and a good versus poor prognosis. However, even Kraepelin noted patients that shared attributes of both illnesses, later termed *schizoaffective* (Kasanin 1933), so that he had difficulty delineating the boundaries of the two illnesses.

The line between affective disorder and schizophrenia has variously included or excluded schizoaffective patients, and has not been well demarcated, changing from decade to decade and country to country in the same decade. Does this inconsistency mean that the division is arbitrary and therefore invalid? Is there really only one illness with differing manifestations, or are the boundaries unclear for other reasons, such as our present, imprecise ways of quantifying mental

We thank Dr. William Coryell for comments on the manuscript and Jeanne Mullen for expert secretarial assistance.

61

illness? The question becomes more important with development of specific treatments that may be effective for one illness and not another. (The fact that treatment specificities exist supports the existence of different illnesses.) The debate here is relevant to all types of psychiatric diagnosis since many symptoms are shared by what are conceived of as "different" illnesses. Do symptoms in common imply a common etiology or pathophysiology?

Since proximal etiologies are largely unknown in psychiatry, the major problem is what constitutes an autonomous disease. To address this, a medical or disease model may be used. The medical model can be conceived as one that focuses on the causes of maladaptive and abnormal behaviors, rather than the behaviors themselves, as constituting the "true" disease. In other words, the behaviors are *symptoms* of disease, rather than disease itself. It is traditional to divide the field of mental illness, as with any other disease, into four major areas: etiology, pathology, epidemiology, and therapy (Scheff 1967). When applying the medical model, psychiatric illnesses are like physical illnesses. They show clusters of symptoms called syndromes, which are named by specific and technical terms. Under these circumstances, research is then accomplished with the implicit understanding that finding the etiology will ultimately lead to an effective treatment (Macklin 1973; Sahakian 1970). The medical model has been criticized as being fundamentally untrue and producing undesirable consequences for those individuals diagnosed as mentally ill (Szasz 1961). However, these criticisms have been adequately addressed elsewhere (Macklin 1973) and are beyond the scope of this chapter.

There are a number of classes of variables involved in the medical model. These would include such identifying characteristics as race, sex, and age of onset. Demographic variables might be of value because population circumstances may be related to the occurrence of an illness. Other variables include the presence of specific symptom clusters, precipitating factors, abnormal laboratory findings, and illness-specific variables (e.g., remitting or episodic versus chronic, or restitution to wellness versus the presence of residual symptoms). Another useful variable is the family history, which suggests a distal, but not a proximal, etiology, since a genetic or familial background does not identify a pathophysiology. Finally, other notable variables are preexisting personality disorders and response to treatment.

Having accumulated data, the next step is a differential diagnosis attempting to separate similar illnesses from each other on the basis of these variables. Ordinarily in psychiatry, the problem in diagnosis occurs because there are many illnesses that manifest themselves by similar clinical symptoms over time. Looked at another way, there are no pathognomonic symptoms in psychiatry. Any symptom may comprise part of a given syndrome, although some may be seen more or less frequently. For instance, the presence of a depressed mood does not define an illness. It may occur as an integral part of almost any psychopathology or as a secondary phenomenon (Coryell 1988). Similarly, the presence of delusions does not make for a specific diagnosis, although they may occur more frequently in conjunction with a specific diagnosis. In short, diagnosis based on the presence or absence of a certain single symptom is only slightly better than flipping a coin (Coryell et al. 1982; Johnson, 1981; Pope and Lipinski 1978; Winokur et al. 1985).

As a result of the lack of specificity, it has been proposed that "functional psychosis" be considered a spectrum with "pure" affective illness at one end and "pure" schizophrenia at the other. A severity continuum runs in parallel from unipolar depression to schizophrenia. In the middle would be a large group of schizoaffective patients exhibiting varying degrees of symptoms from the ends (Beck 1967). This proposition that psychiatric nosology return to a "pre-Kraepelinian" form has received some support from other researchers and will be reviewed below.

ESTABLISHING DIAGNOSTIC VALIDITY OF AFFECTIVE DISORDER AND SCHIZOPHRENIA

Robins and Guze (1970) presented an approach to the establishment of distinct homogeneous syndromes using the medical model. They discussed five phases in the establishment of such syndromes. The first of these was to evaluate the clinical picture, and second to add specific laboratory findings. Next, they suggested a differential diagnosis to separate illnesses with similar presentations from one another as best as possible. Having gone through these phases, the diagnostic syndrome was validated by use of follow-up data and family history material. This method intuitively makes good sense, but it does contain an a priori supposition: that we have a reasonably good idea about diagnoses with which to start. In fact, this is probably true, although not everyone would agree. Obviously, these phases have not been completed for any psychiatric illness to date. Thus it may be valuable to assess diagnosis in psychiatry from a position of no prior knowledge and work forward from there.

For the definition of "new" psychiatric illnesses or "new" conditions that have not been differentiated before, the phases approach may not be sufficient. Another set of principles useful for validating disease concepts in psychiatry is delineated by Cloninger et al. (1985), who list a logical progression from clinical syndrome, through discrete clinical disorder, to pathophysiological entity (Table 1). Each of these levels is increasingly restrictive, with "disease entity" requiring established pathophysiology, a step beyond any psychiatric illness at present.

The kinds of information available that are relevant to distinguishing illnesses include the number of episodes or number of hospitalizations a patient has in a given time. Also, by evaluating symptom clusters, we might look at how many "first-rank" symptoms or how many depressive symptoms the individual shows, or how many antisocial types of behavior are characteristic. In addition, depressive symptoms are ubiquitous and repeatedly seen as secondary phenomena in almost all psychiatric illnesses (Coryell 1988). On the other hand, the presence of formal thought disorder symptoms or first-rank symptoms of schizophrenia are less frequent, and therefore much more usable for separation of clinical entities. When these data are placed within the schema listed, it is clear that no psychiatric diagnosis fulfills all requirements for disease entity, although some syndromes appear to be approaching this point.

Table 1. A Schema for Levels of Disease Concept with Criteria for Each Level

Clinical syndrome	Discrete clinical disorder	Pathophysiological entity
Clinically distinguishable from other syndromes	Operational criteria for syndrome	Identified risk factors
Intercorrelated symptom cluster	Clearly identified syndrome borders	Pathophysiological explanation of symptoms and course
Clinical picture is consistent and stable		Specification of pathway from risk factors to pathophysiology

Note. Adapted from Cloninger et al. (1985).

Statistical Analyses to Discriminate Affective Disorder from Schizophrenia

Implicit in this chapter is the view that the medical model is useful in diagnosis and in separating out autonomous diseases. The question that arises is how it might be used, and how many findings are necessary to have confidence in the fact that it defines an autonomous disease. No symptom is pathognomonic for a specific illness, as noted above; rather we deal with various characteristics that are more frequently seen in one diagnosis and less frequently in another. Frequently, the variables that we use are continuous rather than categorical. Often we can convert continuous variables into categorical variables by classifying their presence or absence or whether they are above or below the mean, but these transformations cause a loss of information. Since the classification systems applied to psychiatry patients are categorical, it is assumed that the illnesses are indeed discrete. This assumption has been questioned (Crow 1986), but can be supported by data, as will be reviewed below.

In a clinical population composed of two or more entities, we might employ a "break-point" model to discriminate these entities (Barlow et al. 1972; Maxwell 1961). A diagram illustrating this is presented in Figure 1a. In this example, the risk of illness in relatives is plotted against the age of the proband, yielding a function that assumes a continuous, smooth line if one entity exists, and a sharply discontinuous function if two populations exist within the sample. The break-point model would work best if one plotted a possible etiological function (e.g., specific family history, ventricular size, dexamethasone suppression test) against a clinical function (e.g., number of schizophrenic symptoms, number of episodes, age of onset). The question that arises is how many significant break-points are needed to allow one to be confident that one has described an autonomous illness or a specific clinical diagnosis. In other words, how many of the characteristics used in a medical model have to show some evidence of a significant break-point before assuming an autonomous illness? Essentially this will turn out to be a convention in the same sense that the .05 level in statistics is assumed to be a reasonable definition of statistical significance, or a logarithm of the odds of linkage (LOD) score of 3 in linkage studies in genetics defines an acceptable statistical basis for assuming linkage between two genetic loci. Unfortunately, the convention for how many break-points are needed to define an autonomous illness is as yet undetermined.

Break-point data can be plotted in another way, looking for non-linear relationships indicating discontinuity (Figure 1b). Another way of viewing the data is to plot the number of cases against a symptom, or cluster of symptoms, and look for so-called points of rarity. An illustration of this is shown in Figure 2, with the solid line revealing a bimodal distribution and the broken line showing a unimodal distribution, indicating two entities or one entity, respectively, within a population. These are both ways of evaluating whether or not there is a logical cut-off point in a series of variables that can be utilized to segregate populations, if differences exist between two populations.

There are some characteristic curves that have been looked for with the break-point model. Hopkinson and Ley (1969), the first to apply this analysis to psychiatry, studied affective disorders and reported a curve similar to the solid line in Figure 1a for affective disorders in relatives plotted against age of onset of illness. The interesting finding was that of a highly significant deviation of the data from a purely linear falloff with increasing age. This illustrates the poten-

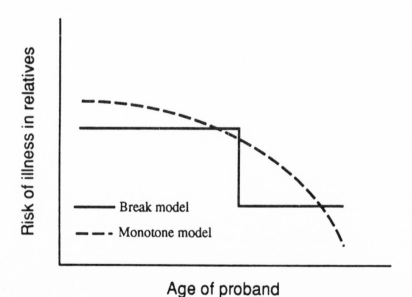

Age of proband

Figure 1a. The break-point model—shows how the break-point model differs from a monotonal, or continuum, model when age of proband is plotted against the risk of illness in relatives. The break-point model is best suited to the plots of a clinical variable versus a possible etiological agent.

tiality of this type of analysis to detect two different types of conditions within a sample presenting similar symptoms. Cadoret et al. (1977) used the break-point model to illustrate that there are probably two types of depressed patients in a group of female depressives.

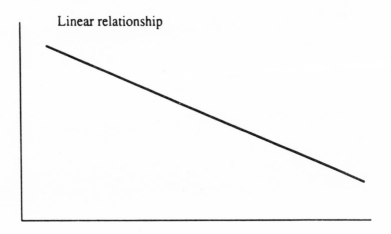

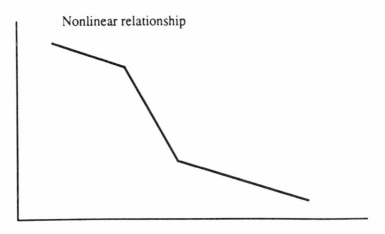

Figure 1b. The break-point model—linearizes the model to show a linear relationship for the continuum model and a "break," or nonlinear, relationship in the break-point model. The break-point model is best suited to the plots of a clinical variable versus a possible etiological agent.

In the exploration of the boundary between affective disorder and schizophrenia (if there is a boundary), this type of analysis has been discussed (Kendell 1982). However, as with most research endeavors in psychiatry, inconsistent results have been obtained.

Kendell and Gourlay (1970) applied a discriminate function analysis to a series of patients and arrived at a trimodal distribution based on presenting symptomatology, with the addition of sex, age, presence of prior episodes, and previous time in hospital. No point of rarity was found. This admittedly ambiguous distribution may likely be due to the absence of items assessing "response to treatment, the extent of recovery, and the subsequence of occurrence of further episodes, or of progressive deterioration" (Kendell and Gourlay 1970, p. 265)—all important factors in Kraepelin's original distinction.

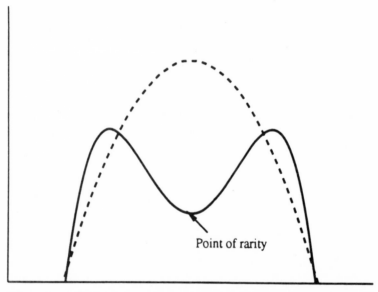

Figure 2. The unimodal versus bimodal curve, with a point-of-rarity in the center of the bimodal curve. The center of the distribution would be patients with schizoaffective disorder, with patients with affective disorder and schizophrenics at either end. Symptom clusters characterizing affective disorder and schizophrenia can be sorted into a bimodal distribution with a point-of-rarity in the center. With a continuum of illness (unimodal distribution), one would expect greater numbers of persons with "mixed" or "schizoaffective" states than with diagnoses at the ends of the continuum (i.e., affective disorder and schizophrenia).

Kraepelin emphasized course of illness as the single most powerful discriminator in the manic-depressive illness–dementia praecox dichotomy. Kendell and Brockington (1980) later applied the more powerful technique of looking for discontinuities in linearized relationships between symptomatology and outcome. The patients from the 1970 sample were followed up an average of 6.5 years later and evaluated on eight different indices of outcome. An essentially linear relationship (see Figure 1b) was found between each of the indices and presenting symptomatology, so no discontinuities were found. This does not prove a lack of separateness between affective disorder and schizophrenia, but certainly does not support this distinction either. The lack of a positive result is not synonymous with a negative result. In other words, the two illnesses may still be distinct, but this view is not supported by these data.

A nine-variable diagnostic measure was developed for discriminating schizophrenia from primary affective disorder by means of a discriminate function analysis and cross-validated by a jackknife procedure that "correctly" classified 9 of 10 patients (Fowler et al. 1980). This suggests that discriminate analysis based on symptomatology can be successful in making the distinction between affective disorder and schizophrenia. This analysis can and does form a point of rarity, if only the proper items are assessed. In a more rigorous study, Cloninger et al. (1985) used discriminate function analysis to distinguish schizophrenia from all other psychiatric diagnoses, as well as from normals. Using the Kendell and Brockington (1980) definition of a discrete disorder, a point of rarity was established; that is, a bimodal distribution between schizophrenics and other patients was demonstrated. In addition, schizophrenic diagnoses increased in nonlinear fashion when a critical number of schizophrenic features were combined. Their success, in contrast to Kendell and Gourlay (1970) and Kendell and Brockington (1980), was attributed to the use of *fewer* discriminate variables than the earlier studies. It is of interest that these variables were quite similar to those identified by Kendell and Gourlay as most characteristic of schizophrenia, but they were not diluted by the use of other less powerful discriminators such as depressed mood, which occurs frequently in schizophrenics (Guze et al. 1983; Johnson 1981; Roy 1981).

Family and Follow-Up Studies

Following the criteria of Robins and Guze (1970), we have at this point confirmed the presence of a clinical picture: a constellation of symptoms that identifies and separates schizophrenia from affective disorder. The next phase was to assign laboratory findings that would enhance the discrimination. Unfortunately, we are unable to pursue this further since it has not been demonstrated that any test can distinguish the two illnesses. There are a number of interesting leads, however. So-called markers of illness have proliferated in recent years; for example, smooth eye pursuit abnormalities have been noted in schizophrenics to a greater extent than in other mentally ill patients (Holzman et al. 1984). Abnormalities in the dexamethasone suppression test that may be able to discriminate between schizophrenic and affective patients have been noted (Coryell 1984). In addition to these examples, there are a great many others that show promise, but it must be emphasized that none can significantly bolster our position that schizophrenia and affective disorder are discrete, separate entities.

The family and follow-up studies, on the other hand, provide highly significant evidence supporting the separation of these two illnesses. If it can be shown, for example, that the first-degree relatives of patients with schizophrenia exhibit high rates of schizophrenia with "normal" rates of affective disorder, the justification of separating the two entities is strengthened considerably. The reverse must also be true: first-degree relatives of patients with affective disorder must have high rates of affective illness and low, or "normal" rates of schizophrenia. If these conditions are not fulfilled, that does not mean that there is only one illness; disease entities do not necessarily run in families. If these patterns are noted, however, it is consistent with the distinction of the two illnesses.

Long-term follow-up studies can demonstrate that symptom patterns remain stable over a period of years, which is requisite for claiming the existence of two entities. If an individual was noted to switch from one illness to another, the separation is weakened. This criterion is necessary, but not sufficient. In fact, all of the varied approaches to illustrating the distinction between the two illnesses are necessary but not sufficient. Tsuang et al. (1981) showed that the diagnoses of affective disorder and schizophrenia remain stable over a period of 30 to 40 years. Guze et al. (1983) also blindly followed up a large cohort of patients for 6 to 12 years and showed that the two diagnoses were stable. It is clear that these diagnoses can be assigned in such a manner as to ensure long-term stability.

In the same article, Guze et al. (1983) interviewed a large number of first-degree relatives to assess the rates of affective disorder and schizophrenia in families of probands with these two diagnoses (among others). Affective disorder was found in only 2.7% of the relatives of schizophrenics versus 6.8% of the relatives of nonschizophrenic probands (a grouping of patients with affective, antisocial, and anxiety disorders and alcoholism). Even more significant was the fact that there was no increase in the rates of affective illness in relatives of schizophrenics who suffered intercurrent episodes of depression. This is illustrated in Table 2. It should be noted that the morbid risk for affective disorder was actually higher among relatives of probands who had schizophrenia without an affective syndrome than among relatives of schizophrenic patients who exhibited a depressive syndrome. This cannot be reconciled with the view of a continuum of illness from affective to schizophrenic. If a continuum existed, schizophrenic patients with depression should show more affective illness in their relatives.

Further evidence of the two illnesses "breeding true" is given by Tsuang et al. (1980), who blindly interviewed more than 1,500 relatives of schizophrenic and affective patients and controls. Morbidity risks for schizophrenia were significantly higher among relatives of schizophrenic patients than among relatives of depressed patients, and risk for depression was greater among relatives of depressed probands when compared to schizophrenic patients. Therefore, it can be shown that the two illnesses sort separately in families, confirming their disrelation.

THE PROBLEM WITH SCHIZOAFFECTIVE PATIENTS

If a continuum of psychosis exists, one should expect that the center of a unimodal distribution (see Figure 2) should contain at least as many, if not more, members than the "tail" diagnosis: in this case schizoaffective disorder, affective disorder, and schizophrenia, respectively. How one defines *schizoaffective* plays a large part in determining the prevalence and family history of the disorder. Using Research Diagnostic Criteria (RDC), Weissman et al. (1978) as-

Table 2. Family Study of Schizophrenia

	Patients with schizophrenia without affective syndrome (N = 19)	Patients with schizophrenia with affective syndrome (N = 25)
Relatives (N)	45	66
Morbid risk of schizophrenia	6.0%	9.1%
Morbid risk of affective disorder	6.7%	0%

Note. Adapted from Guze et al. (1983).

signed diagnoses to a sample of adults in New Haven and found no schizoaffective patients versus 4.3% with major depression and 0.4% with schizophrenia. While there are other studies showing higher rates of schizoaffective patients, it is fair to say that the very existence of the disorder has been questioned.

Family studies have confirmed that operationally defined affective illness and schizophrenia "breed true." No such consensus exists, however, for those patients that are classified in the unclear area between the two diagnoses. A large number of well-controlled, rigorous studies have concluded that schizoaffective disorder is, in general, more closely related to affective illness than to schizophrenia (for review, see Rogers and Winokur 1988), depending on diagnostic criteria. One of the clearest findings in this area is by Pope et al. (1980), who found rates of schizophrenia in families of patients with schizoaffective and affective disorders to be equal (far less than rates in families of schizophrenics), and rates of affective illness equal in families of patients with schizoaffective and affective disorders (far greater than rates noted in schizophrenics). There is a wide diversity of findings in this area, however, probably based on the diversity of definitions used to define cohorts for study.

Brockington and Leff (1979) showed a very low mutual concordance of 0.19 between eight definitions of *schizoaffective* and concluded that "it seems unlikely that the schizo-affective concept corresponds to anything well-demarcated in the natural state" (p. 96). It should be noted that 4.5% of hospital admissions fulfilled requirements for three (or more) definitions in their sample. In conclusion, schizoaffective patients do not exhibit a unique inheritance, but instead have familial lines very similar to either patients with affective disorder or with schizophrenia, depending on how the probands are diagnosed. It is the overreliance on clinical presentation and underreliance on clinical course that result in the schizoaffective diagnosis; the individual patients appear to sort into one category or the other if followed over time. This difficulty is reminiscent of the debate concerning the existence of a continuum of psychosis and has its roots in the phenomenology of mental illness. Once pathophysiologies are clarified, the answers to the questions of where to draw the lines will be readily apparent.

Possible Pathophysiology?

Despite the voluminous literature on the many abnormalities of function in those patients suffering from mental illness, no etiology has emerged. A review of all existing hypotheses concerning such etiology is not appropriate here. However, there is a recent mechanism proposed for a neural system that incorporates much of what is known about pathophysiology into an integrated theory underlying both schizophrenia and affective disorder. The theory is modeled after current understanding of the pathophysiologies of movement disorders, and involves interactions of limbic cortex (LCX), nucleus accumbens (NAC), ventral pallidum (VPA), ventral tegmentum (VTG), and the dorsomedial nucleus of the thalamus (DMN). Projections to and from these structures form a series of loops, in analogy to basal ganglia circuitry (Figure 3) (Swerdlow and Koob 1987).

The LCX-DMN-LCX loop is proposed to maintain a continuous stream of emotional and cognitive impulses, in a positive feedback manner, modulated by inhibition from the VPA. The VPA is itself inhibited by the NAC, which is activated by the LCX. Inhibition of the NAC would in turn disinhibit the VPA and allow for cognitive switching. The sequence of two inhibitory steps is capable of exciting the cortico-thalamic circuitry, and may be promoted through excitatory inputs from the LCX to the NAC. Cortical neurons could therefore promote their own activity, maintaining a cognitive set.

Disturbances of cognitive "filtering" processes have been proposed as mechanisms underlying the thought disorder of psychosis. In this model, psychosis is thought to occur due to excessive dopamine-mediated inhibition of the NAC, leading to increased activity of the VPA, with disrupted filtering (or focusing) capacity, allowing increased switching. Deficient dopamine input (from VTG) to the NAC would result in increased VPA activity with an inability

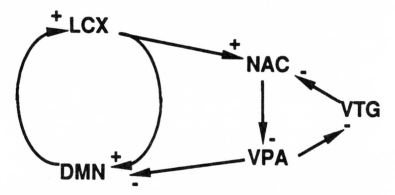

Figure 3. The neural circuitry proposed to underlie psychosis and depression. LCX = limbic cortex; NAC = nucleus accumbens; VPA = ventral pallidum; VTG = ventral tegmentum; DMN = dorsomedial nucleus. Adapted from Swerdlow and Koob (1987).

to switch or initiate new cognitive sets, a symptom of depression (Swerdlow and Koob 1987).

This model is a simplification of complex interactions, both in terms of anatomical projections and pharmacological action; nonetheless, it provides a framework to incorporate a variety of disparate, fractured data. If a mechanism such as this underlies mental illness, it is easy to see how the two illnesses could present with overlapping symptoms. All mental illnesses have in common a limited repertoire of behavioral manifestations, perhaps mediated by common central nervous system structures. In this scenario, it would be expected that distinct illnesses share common symptomatology to some extent. Swerdlow and Koob (1987) stated that "the goal of this approach is not to understand the etiology of a single disease, but rather to study how dysfunction in a single brain system contributes to similar behavioral abnormalities in different disease processes" (p. 202).

CONCLUSION

The unitary view of mental illness was popular prior to the work of Kraepelin. Since that time, affective disorder and schizophrenia have been thought of as separate disease entities, presumably with distinct pathophysiologies. In the absence of identified etiologies, the continuum view of mental illness (affective disorder and schizophrenia in particular) has resurfaced in an effort to explain what was perceived as anomalous research findings. The most disturbing of these findings is the inability of Kendell and co-workers to identify symptom clusters that distinguish the two illnesses. The view of psychosis as a continuum has been championed recently by Crow (1986, 1987), who outlined the support for the continuum as essentially the absence of proof of the binary "two-entity" concept. This view can be questioned by a careful review of the literature on affective disorder, schizophrenia, and schizoaffective disorder.

As discussed above, it has been shown that discriminate function analysis can separate the two illnesses based on symptomatology (Cloninger et al. 1985). A point of rarity was demonstrated between the two syndromes. In the same study, bimodality of outcome was evinced for schizophrenia against all other psychiatric diagnoses. Tsuang et al. (1980) has provided convincing evidence that affective disorder and schizophrenia breed true. Furthermore, Tsuang et al. (1981) and Guze et al. (1983) showed that the diagnoses of affective disorder and schizophrenia were quite stable over long periods, provided the diagnoses were made using established criteria. Lastly, schizoaffective disorder, the diagnosis in the middle of the continuum, has not been shown to be a valid diagnosis based on family and follow-up studies (Rogers and Winokur 1988) and is not present in significant amounts in the general population (Weissman et al. 1978). To expect perfect homogeneity among patient populations in terms of phenomenology or follow-up is unfounded, especially in the absence of a defined etiology. However, current definitions of affective disorder and schizophrenia do a plausible job of delineating two distinct clinical syndromes, and very likely two different disease states.

REFERENCES

Barlow R, Bartholomew D, Bremmer J, et al: Statistical Inference under Order Restrictions. New York, John Wiley & Sons, 1972

Beck AT: Depression: Clinical, Experimental and Theoretical Aspects. New York, Harper & Row, 1967

Brockington IF, Leff JP: Schizo-affective psychosis: definitions and incidence. Psychol Med 9:91–99, 1979

Cadoret RJ, Woolson R, Winokur G: The relationship of age of onset in unipolar affective disorder to risk of alcoholism and depression in parents. J Psychiatr Res 13:137–142, 1977

Cloninger CR, Martin RL, Guze SB, et al: Diagnosis and prognosis in schizophrenia. Arch Gen Psychiatry 42:15–25, 1985

Coryell W: The use of laboratory tests in psychiatric diagnosis: the DST as an example. Psychiatr Dev 3:139–159, 1984

Coryell W: Secondary depression, in Psychiatry. Edited by Michels R, Cavenar JO, Brodie HKH, et al. Philadelphia, Lippincott, 1988

Coryell W, Tsuang MT, McDaniel J: Psychotic features in major depression. Is mood congruence important? J Affective Disord 4:227–236, 1982

Crow TJ: The continuum of psychosis and its implication for the structure of the gene. Br J Psychiatry 149:419–429, 1986

Crow TJ: Psychosis as a continuum and the virogene concept. Br Med Bull 43:754–767, 1987

Fowler RC, Liskow BI, Tanna VL, et al: Schizophrenia: primary affective disorder discrimination: I, development of a data-based diagnostic index. Arch Gen Psychiatry 37:811–814, 1980

Guze SB, Cloninger R, Martin RL, et al: A follow-up and family study of schizophrenia. Arch Gen Psychiatry 40:1273–1276, 1983

Holzman PS, Solomon CM, Levin S, et al: Pursuit eye movement dysfunctions in schizophrenia: family evidence for specificity. Arch Gen Psychiatry 41:136–139, 1984

Hopkinson G, Ley P: A genetic study of affective disorder. Br J Psychiatry 115:917–922, 1969

Johnson DAW: Studies of depressive symptoms in schizophrenia: I, the prevalence of depression and its possible causes. Br J Psychiatry 139:89–101, 1981

Kasanin J: The acute schizoaffective psychoses. Am J Psychiatry 13:97–126, 1933

Kendell RE: The choice of diagnostic criteria for biological research. Arch Gen Psychiatry 39:1334–1339, 1982

Kendell RE, Brockington IF: The identification of disease entities and the relationship between schizophrenic and affective psychoses. Br J Psychiatry 137:324–331, 1980

Kendell RE, Gourlay J: The clinical distinction between the affective psychoses and schizophrenia. Br J Psychiatry 117:261–266, 1970

Macklin R: The medical model in psychoanalysis and psychotherapy. Compr Psychiatry 14:49–69, 1973

Maxwell AE: Analyzing Qualitative Data. London, Methuen, 1961

Pope HG, Lipinski JF: Diagnosis in schizophrenia and manic-depressive illness. Arch Gen Psychiatry 35:811–828, 1978

Pope HG, Lipinski JF, Cohen BM, et al: "Schizoaffective disorder": an invalid diagnosis? A comparison of schizoaffective disorder, schizophrenia, and affective disorder. Am J Psychiatry 137:921–927, 1980

Robins E, Guze SB: Establishment of diagnostic validity in psychiatric illness: its application to schizophrenia. Am J Psychiatry 126:983–987, 1970

Rogers KL, Winokur G: The genetics of schizo-affective disorder and the schizophrenia spectrum, in Handbook of Schizophrenia, Vol 3: Nosology, Epidemiology, and Genetics. Edited by Tsuang MT, Simpson JC. Amsterdam, Elsevier, 1988

Roy A: Depression in the course of chronic undifferentiated schizophrenia. Arch Gen Psychiatry 38:296–297, 1981

Sahakian WS (ed): Psychopathology Today. Itasca, Ill, Peacock, 1970

Scheff TJ (ed): Mental Illness and Social Processes. New York, Harper & Row, 1967

Swerdlow NR, Koob GF: Dopamine, schizophrenia, mania, and depression: toward a unified hypothesis of cortico-striato-pallido-thalamic function. Behavioral and Brain Sciences 10:197–245, 1987

Szasz TS: The Myth of Mental Illness. New York, Hoeber-Harper, 1961

Tsuang MT, Winokur G, Crowe RR: Morbidity risks of schizophrenia and affective disorders among first degree relatives of patients with schizophrenia, mania, depression, and surgical conditions. Br J Psychiatry 137:497–504, 1980

Tsuang MT, Woolson RF, Winokur G, et al: Stability of psychiatric diagnosis: schizophrenia and affective disorders followed up over a 30-40 year period. Arch Gen Psychiatry 38:535–539, 1981

Weissman MM, Myers JK, Harding PS: Psychiatric disorders in a U.S. urban community: 1975-1976. Am J Psychiatry 135:459–462, 1978

Winokur G, Scharfetter C, Angst J: The diagnostic value in assessing mood congruence in delusions and hallucinations and their relationship to the affective state. Eur Arch Psychiatry Neurol Sci 234:299–302, 1985

Chapter 5

The Question of a Genetic Continuum for Schizophrenia and Affective Disorder

Timothy J. Crow, M.B., Ph.D.

Chapter 5

The Question of a Genetic Continuum for Schizophrenia and Affective Disorder

A role for genetic factors in psychosis is now generally conceded, although opinions differ on whether they are sometimes present and sometimes absent, or generally present and additive with other etiological factors. That genetic factors are by themselves sufficient cannot easily be ruled out. Karlsson (1970) pointed out that adoption away from relatives with schizophrenia does not decrease the individual's risk of the disease. This suggests the environment contributes little. Recent estimates of the heritability of schizophrenia (McGue et al. 1983; Rao et al. 1981) have yielded figures well in excess of 50%, and a residual component is often attributed to the environment. However, it remains to be established that this component is indeed related to identifiable environmental factors rather than to error and to the genetic assumptions on which the calculations are based. It is often argued that discordance for psychosis in monozygotic twins establishes that environmental factors are sometimes necessary. However, this argument ignores the possibility of somatic mutation (well established in the immune system), and the possibility to which Boklage (1977) drew attention that discordance is related to factors in development responsible for differences (e.g., in cerebral laterality) between the twins. Such differences, although ill-understood, seem unlikely to be environmental in any simple sense. They may be random, or determined by events at the stage at which a single zygote gives rise to two embryos.

Contemporary classifications of psychiatric disease owe much to

This chapter was adapted from Br Med Bull 43:754–767, 1987, and Br J Psychiatry 149:419–429, 1986.

Kraepelin (1899). At the end of the last century, he distinguished the organic from the functional psychoses and, in the latter category, separated manic-depressive insanity from dementia praecox (schizophrenia). The separation was achieved on the basis of outcome: an episodic course with recovery from individual episodes was regarded as characteristic of manic-depressive illness, whereas in dementia praecox an element of persistence and even progression was to be expected. Although exceptions are recognized, this generalization has survived relatively unchallenged.

KRAEPELIN'S BINARY THEORY

Kraepelin's "binary" view (sometimes referred to as the "two-entities principle") has dominated subsequent work to the extent that schizophrenia and manic-depressive illness are widely regarded as separate diseases, each with a different genetic background, treatment, and outcome (Gershon and Rieder 1980; Loranger 1981). The earlier view (Griesinger 1861; Guislain 1833; Neumann 1859) that there is a unity in the psychoses (the "einheit-psychose") has yielded to common observation that typical cases of manic-depressive illness and schizophrenia have distinct psychopathological features, usually follow their predicted courses, and are associated with an incidence of similar illnesses in first-degree relatives.

This chapter presents an alternative to Kraepelin's binary concept. Doubts about the binary hypothesis arise first from the failure of Kendell and co-workers (Kendell and Brockington 1980; Kendell and Gourlay 1970) to achieve a bimodal separation of the two conditions on the basis of symptoms or outcome. Second, in family studies, two findings indicate that the conditions are more closely related genetically than is generally believed: several investigations have shown an excess of children with schizophrenia among the offspring of parents with affective disorder, and studies of "schizoaffective psychosis" have failed to separate this entity from either affective disorder or schizophrenia (see discussion below).

The alternative concept is that there is a continuum of psychosis extending from pure affective disorder to schizophrenia with the defect state. The existence of such a continuum would imply that the genetic mechanisms postulated to underlie it are subject to more rapid change than is associated with most human genes.

It seems that Kraepelin (1920/1974) himself had doubts about the binary concept:

> Perhaps it is . . . possible to tackle the difficulties which still prevent us from distinguishing reliably between manic-depressive insanity and de-

mentia praecox. No experienced psychiatrist will deny that there is an alarmingly large number of cases in which it seems impossible, in spite of the most careful observation, to make a firm diagnosis. . . . Nevertheless it is becoming increasingly clear that we cannot distinguish satisfactorily between these two illnesses and this brings home the suspicion that our formulation of the problem may be incorrect. (pp. 27–28)

However, he went on:

The great mass of patients who, on the one hand, present irreversible dementing cortical disturbances and, on the other recover with their personality intact, speaks eloquently in support of the fact that there is a real difference here, especially since it is often enough possible to predict the outcome from the clinical syndrome. (p. 28)

LIMITATIONS OF THE BINARY CONCEPT

A persistent problem for the binary view has been the undoubted occurrence of psychoses with both manic-depressive and schizophrenic symptoms. Kasanin (1933) introduced the concept of schizoaffective psychosis and initiated discussion as to whether such illnesses are variants of one or other of the prototypes, or constitute a "third psychosis."

It is generally assumed that "true" schizoaffective psychoses, which cannot be placed in either category, are relatively rare, and that the majority of psychotic illnesses can be classified as either affective or schizophrenic. It would thus be expected that a discriminant function based on the characteristic features would separate the two major conditions with relatively few intermediate cases. In testing this prediction on data from the United States–United Kingdom Diagnostic Project, collected using the Present State Examination and a semi-structured history schedule, Kendell and Gourlay (1970), on the contrary, found a distribution with a maximum of cases at the midpoint between the two typical pictures. A discriminant function that included all those items that best distinguished patients with a project diagnosis of affective disorder from those with a project diagnosis of schizophrenia failed to separate the groups and leave a "region of rarity" between them.

In a further sample of 217, Kendell and Gourlay (1970) again failed to demonstrate bimodality: this time the distribution on the discriminant function was unimodal rather than trimodal. Such findings cast doubt on the common clinical assumption that most cases of psychosis can be relatively easily classified as either affective or schizophrenic.

Kendell and Brockington (1980) later developed a method for

ascertaining a nonlinear relationship between symptomatology and outcome, but were unable to demonstrate such relationships in samples of 127 unselected psychotic and 105 schizoaffective patients. They wrote: "No firm conclusions can be drawn about the relationship between schizophrenic and affective psychoses, though it has to be noted that yet another attempt to demonstrate discontinuity between them has failed" (p. 330).

The diagnostic boundaries of schizophrenia have long been debated. Nuclear symptoms (e.g., thoughts experienced as alien or as auditory hallucinations) were advanced by Schneider (1957) as pathognomonic, but they define a restricted range of illnesses and are not directly related to poor outcome (Bland and Orn 1980). An alternative strategy adopted in recent research criteria—for example, the DSM-III criteria (American Psychiatric Association 1980) and the earlier criteria of Feighner et al. (1972)—is to include duration as a defining feature. Such criteria are successful in predicting outcome. Outcome for the schizoaffective psychoses, whether studied before (Clark and Mallett 1963; Hunt and Appel 1936) or after (Brockington et al. 1980; Croughan et al. 1974) the introduction of operational criteria, is found to be intermediate between schizophrenia and affective disorder. Thus, although bimodality of outcome has been claimed in one study (Cloninger et al. 1985), experience with schizoaffective illness does not appear to support it.

A recent independent challenge to the Kraepelinian viewpoint is the suggestion that the clinical picture in the individual patient is less constant than is often thought. Thus Sheldrick (1975) and Sheldrick et al. (1977) drew attention to a group of patients who presented with apparently typical schizophrenic illness but later suffered from episodes of illness that were affective in form. Conversely, Kendler and Tsuang (1982) reported a pair of monozygotic twins, each of whom progressed from typical affective illness to "process" schizophrenia. They suggested that the progression is genetically determined. Most unexpected, from a Kraepelinian and a genetic viewpoint, is the report of McGuffin et al. (1982) of identical triplets discordant for type of psychosis according to binary typology. Each of these findings appears to be exceptional (although the precise frequency of such exceptions is of considerable interest), as can be seen from the findings of the major studies (e.g., Gershon et al. 1982; Kendler et al. 1985; Tsuang et al. 1980), which document the relative stability of the clinical picture within families.

The two prototypical psychoses share some salient features. Both show a tendency to recur, more striking in the case of manic-depressive psychosis but present also in schizophrenia. Onset before puberty is rare in either case, but the disease can occur at any point in adult life, the mean onset of schizophrenia being earlier (by a decade or more) than affective illness. The lifetime prevalence of both conditions approaches 1%. In neither case have characteristic histopathological changes in the brain been established, although recent neuroradiological (Johnstone et al. 1976) and postmortem studies (Brown et al. 1986) suggest structural changes (e.g., cerebral ventricular enlargement) that are more marked in schizophrenia.

The prophylactic value of medication is established in both conditions: lithium in preventing relapse in affective illness (Davis 1976), and neuroleptic medication in schizophrenia (Davis 1975). Although such drug specificity suggests differences in the underlying disease processes, some schizophrenic illnesses respond to lithium (Biederman et al. 1979; Delva and Letemendia 1986), and, in addition to their efficacy in mania, neuroleptics may be of value in depression (Hollister et al. 1967).

A recent study (Johnstone et al. 1988) reinforces this point. One hundred twenty patients with psychosis (including both affective and schizophrenic types of illness) were randomly allocated to neuroleptic (pimozide), lithium, or combination of pimozide and lithium, and placebo. While lithium was found to have some specificity to affective change, the more substantial benefits of pimozide were as great in patients with predominantly affective pychoses as in those with predominantly schizophrenic psychoses.

Thus no unequivocal demarcation of the functional psychoses can be made on the basis of symptoms, outcome, or response to treatment.

ARE SCHIZOPHRENIA AND AFFECTIVE PSYCHOSIS GENETICALLY RELATED?

It is widely held that the genetic factors that predispose to the two typical psychoses are unrelated. Thus, according to Gershon and Rieder (1980, p. 106): "Evidence from twin and family studies suggests that bipolar manic depressive illness and chronic schizophrenia are distinct entities." According to Reich et al. (1982, p. 159): "The genetic diathesis for affective disorders is independent of that for other psychiatric disorders." Several findings suggest that such conclusions are too dogmatic. Rather, the two conditions appear to be related in a way that reveals something about the genetic mechanisms. Specifically, affective illness in one generation may predispose to schizophrenia in the next.

In a survey of the risk of other psychiatric illness in first-degree relatives of patients with affective disorder, Rosenthal (1970) noted an excess of schizophrenia in children (a mean of 2.3% in five studies), while the risk in parents and siblings remained within the 0.8% lifetime prevalence for the general population. He asked (p. 163): "From the genetic point of view, why should schizophrenia have occurred at all in these families?"

Two studies have examined parent-child pairs in which both members suffered from psychosis (Table 1). Penrose (1968) identified 621 such pairs in a series of 5,456 pairs of relatives with psychiatric disease collected over a period of 18 years in the Ontario mental hospitals. Among the ill children of schizophrenic parents, a diagnosis of schizophrenia preponderated over affective disorder in a ratio of almost 5:1. Among the children of affectively ill parents, the ratio was a little less than 1; schizophrenia was almost as common as affective disorder. In a similar study on the Aberdeen Case Register, Powell et al. (1973) found schizophrenia in the children of schizophrenic parents and affective illness among the children of parents with affective disorder, as expected. However, among the latter, they found that for 10 cases of affective disorder, 15 cases of schizophrenia were also present.

These findings suggest an excess of schizophrenia among the children of affectively ill parents; this seems unlikely to be due to a secular trend toward diagnosing more schizophrenia, or to selective factors (e.g., hospital admission) leading to overinclusion of patients with schizophrenia, as the two samples were collected 30 years apart on either side of the Atlantic, one from inpatient records and the other from a case contact register.

In a series of 25 children of two parents with manic-depressive disorder, Schulz (1940) reported that 7 suffered from affective illness

Table 1. Psychotic Offspring of Psychotic Parents Classified by Diagnosis

Parents	Offspring	
Penrose (1968)	Affective disorder	Schizophrenia
Affective disorder	232	205
Schizophrenia	34	150
Powell et al. (1973)	Manic-depressive psychosis	Schizophrenia
Manic-depressive psychosis	10	15
Schizophrenia	0	9

but 3 suffered from schizophrenia. In applying more restrictive diagnostic criteria to a larger literature, Elsasser (1952) found that, of 169 children of two parents with manic-depressive or atypical psychoses (i.e., with schizophrenia excluded), 18 suffered from definite affective illness and 6 from definite schizophrenia.

Pollock and Malzberg (1940) collected family histories of psychosis over three generations. In relatives from preceding generations (parents, grandparents, uncles, and aunts) of patients with schizophrenia, they found an excess of affective illness: 15 cases of affective illness compared with 11 of schizophrenia (Table 2).

Slater (1953) reported similar findings. In his study of twins, he recorded psychiatric illness in other relatives and found a ratio of affective disorder to schizophrenia particularly high (4:3) in the parents of patients with schizophrenia. The corresponding ratio of 3:5 for siblings similarly showed more affective disorder than would conventionally be expected (Table 2). No excess of schizophrenia was found in the parents or siblings of patients with affective disorder.

In an earlier study of manic-depressive illness (Slater 1936), "a surprising feature had been the number of schizophrenics among the

Table 2.   Psychotic Illness in the Preceding Generations and Siblings of Patients with Affective Disorder or Schizophrenia

Relative group	Proband diagnosis	
	Affective disorder	Schizophrenia
Pollock and Malzberg (1940)	($n = 155$)	($n = 175$)
Preceding generations (parents, uncles, aunts, grandparents)		
Manic-depressive psychosis	7	15
Schizophrenia	3	11
Siblings		
Manic-depressive psychosis	11	2
Schizophrenia	3	8
Slater (1953)	($n = 38$)	($n = 156$)
Parents		
Affective disorder	9	16
Schizophrenia	0	12
Siblings		
Affective Disorder	12	15
Schizophrenia	1	26

children. . . . In 10 of the 15 cases where manic-depressive subjects had been found by Dr. Slater to have schizophrenic children he had been unable to find schizophrenia in other members of the patient's family or that of the husband and wife" (pp. 429–430).

Each of these observations, therefore, is consistent with a one-way movement between generations from affective disorder to schizophrenia. On the basis of his own family studies, Myerson (1925) summarized what he believed to be the inheritance of mental disease:

> That the manic-melancholic diseases are in the main followed by manic-melancholic diseases, but in a certain number, especially of doubtful cases by dementia praecox . . . that the manic-depressive states of involution trend toward manic-depressive and dementia praecox, especially the latter . . . that dementia praecox in an ancestor trends toward dementia praecox in the descendants with a certain scattering incidence of imbecility.

Such a notion is an echo of the concept of the degeneration psychosis as formulated by Morel (1860) and Magnan (1893). As a genetic theory, it is unorthodox, but on the accumulated literature looked at from an intergenerational standpoint, it cannot easily be dismissed.

THE GENETICS OF SCHIZOAFFECTIVE DISORDER

Because of the historical origins of the concept of schizoaffective psychosis and its pivotal position in nosology, particular interest attaches to the genetics involved.

In the largest study at this writing, Angst et al. (1979) found the risk of schizophrenia and affective disorder to be approximately equal in first-degree relatives of schizoaffective probands, and that of schizoaffective illness to be appreciably less than that of either of the prototypical psychoses (Table 3). Two other surveys (Baron et al. 1982; Tsuang et al. 1977) found schizoaffective disorder to be more closely related to affective illness than to schizophrenia. Each group of researchers inferred that schizoaffective illnesses are not genetically separate from the major (particularly affective) psychoses. The conclusion that schizoaffective illness is not a genetic entity was also reached by Tsuang (1979) in a study of pairs of siblings with psychosis. When diagnoses were blindly allocated to the categories of schizophrenia, affective disorder, and schizoaffective disorder, a deficit of schizoaffective × schizoaffective pairs was observed relative to the number of such diagnoses in the sample. Eight schizoaffective × affective, five schizoaffective × schizophrenic, and two schizophrenic × affective pairs were present in a sample of 35 pairs.

The relationship of schizoaffective illness to the affective disorders is illuminated by Gershon et al.'s (1982) study with modified Research Diagnostic Criteria of 1,254 relatives of patients with major affective disorder: "These data were compatible with the different affective disorders representing thresholds on a continuum of underlying multifactorial vulnerability. In this model schizoaffective illness represents greatest vulnerability, followed by bipolar . . . then unipolar (affective) illness" (p. 1157). These authors thus espouse a continuum concept that extends up to schizoaffective illness but excludes schizophrenia.

It is of interest that in Gershon et al.'s (1982) investigation there was an excess ($p < .001$) of schizophrenia among the relatives of patients with schizoaffective illnesses in comparison with those having other types of affective illness. Also of note with respect to intergenerational effects is the finding that the risk of schizoaffective illness in the siblings of the generation succeeding the proband is increased (at 3.9% age-corrected lifetime risk) in comparison with siblings of the proband (0.8%) and siblings of members of the generation preceding the proband (0%).

If schizoaffective disorder does not breed true and has a relationship—as suggested by Baron et al. (1982), Gershon et al. (1982), and Tsuang et al. (1977)—to affective disorder, the question arises whether an excess of schizoaffective illness (or affective disorder) is seen among first-degree relatives of patients with schizophrenia when schizophrenia is narrowly defined as in recent operational criteria. Kendler et al. (1985) reanalyzed a consecutive series of 510 patients

Table 3. Risk of Psychosis in First-Degree Relatives of Probands with Schizoaffective Psychoses: Percentages of Relatives Affected

Type of psychosis	Angst et al. (1979) ($n = 150$)	Tsuang et al. (1977) ($n = 52$)	Baron et al. (1982) ($n = 50$) SA-A	Baron et al. (1982) ($n = 50$) SA-S
Schizophrenia	5.26	0.9	0	4.1
Schizoaffective psychosis	2.97	—	3.2	1.4
Affective psychosis	6.70	11.8	28.1	10.9

Note. Schizoaffective illness was subdivided into mainly affective (SA-A) and mainly schizophrenic (SA-S) in the investigation of Baron et al. 1982.

with a chart diagnosis of schizophrenia from the Iowa hospitals with the DSM-III criteria, and compared rates of illness in the relatives of 332 patients with a DSM-III diagnosis of schizophrenia with those in relatives of 318 surgical controls. In their analysis of personal interview or hospital records, these authors found that while the risk of affective disorder was not significantly increased, the risk of schizo-affective disorder and atypical psychosis was ($p < .01$ or less). Even with a restricted definition of schizophrenia, therefore, no "genetically pure" syndrome is isolated, and a relationship with the schizo-affective spectrum remains.

It is also of interest that an earlier study (Tsuang et al. 1980) of the Iowa series, which did not allow schizoaffective diagnoses, supported the distinction between schizophrenia and affective disorder "although the distinction between schizophrenia and mania was not clear-cut" (p. 497). Subtyping of paranoid and nonparanoid schizophrenia and of unipolar and bipolar affective disorder on the basis of familial associations was not supported. These conclusions do not appear to rule out a continuum concept.

From the above studies, it seems that schizoaffective illness occurs in the relatives of patients with both schizophrenia and affective disorder, even when these illnesses are restrictively defined. The findings of a recent study by Gershon et al. (1988) are of particular interest and significantly modify this group's earlier conclusion that schizoaffective disorder is no more than the extremity of an affective continuum. In an examination of 237 relatives of 48 patients with chronic psychosis diagnosed as either schizophrenia or schizoaffective disorder, they concluded that:

> There was no tendency for schizoaffective diagnosis or acute psychoses to aggregate separately from schizophrenia. Increased incidence of bipolar disorder was found in relatives of patients with schizoaffective disorder but not in relatives of patients with schizophrenia. Incidence of major affective disorder (bipolar and unipolar) was increased in relatives of patients with both types [schizoaffective and acute] of psychoses. (p. 328)

These conclusions, it seems, are entirely compatible with the notion that while typical affective disorder and typical schizophrenia are distinct symptom patterns, they are at the ends of a continuum that includes a range of intermediate forms of psychosis, each of which is interrelated on a genetic basis. There is no point at which a line can be consistently drawn to demarcate one group of illnesses from the other.

A number of studies have related outcome in schizophrenia to incidence of atypical or affective psychoses in relatives. Thus Kant (1942) studied family histories of 50 deteriorated and 50 recovered schizophrenic patients and found that while overall rates of psychosis were similar in the two groups, the ratio of schizophrenia to affective disorder was 5:1 in the former and 1:5 in the latter. However, he noted that "none of the manic-depressive patients among the relatives of the recovered group actually belong to the manic-depressive nucleus. . . . There are several whose clinical pictures remind one strongly of the corresponding atypical types in the recovered schizophrenic group" (p. 186). With a parallel strategy, Kendler and Hays (1983) studied patients with schizophrenia diagnosed by DSM-III criteria, and identified a group of 18 with a first-degree relative with unipolar affective disorder and 10 with a relative with bipolar affective disorder, whom they compared with a group of 98 with no affective disorder in first-degree relatives. These authors commented on their own and some other authors' apparently high rates of affective disorder in relatives as "probably representative of most families of schizophrenics" (p. 954). Patients with a family history of affective disorder were more likely to have suffered from affective symptoms on follow-up. Kendler and Hays concluded that "even when DSM-III criteria are met, hesitation is indicated in diagnosing schizophrenia in patients with a first degree relative with bipolar illness" (p. 951). Similarly, Pope and Lipinski (1978) reviewed 15 studies of "good prognosis," "remitting," and "recovered" schizophrenia and "atypical," "schizophreniform," and "schizoaffective" psychoses. They drew attention to the high frequencies of affective illness in the relatives. They warned that "over-reliance on [clinical] symptoms alone results in over-diagnosis of schizophrenia and under-diagnosis of affective disorder, particularly mania. This compromises both clinical treatment and research" (p. 811).

Underlying the views of Kendler and Hays (1983) and Pope and Lipinski (1978) is the conviction that the binary concept is correct, but that the location of the borderline has strayed from its position of Kraepelinian rectitude; if this borderline were replaced, symptoms and outcome would separate in the prescribed bimodal manner. The work of Kendell and Gourlay (1970) and Kendell and Brockington (1980) gives no support to this notion. Moreover, in the recent literature, the border has moved far in one direction and then far in the other, without finding a satisfactory resting place. It is clear from the work of Kendler and Hays (1983) and Kendler et al. (1985) that the DSM-III criteria do not locate it. It has to be considered that no such natural resting place exists.

From the above literature it seems that schizoaffective illness occurs in the relatives of patients with both schizophrenia and affective disorder even when these illnesses are restrictively defined. Unless schizoaffective disorder can be partitioned into schizophrenic and affective types of illness (and since the concept originated in the failure of such an enterprise, this seems unlikely), parsimony requires the conclusion that schizoaffective disorder is but the bridge between affective disorders and schizophrenia. The psychoses constitute a genetic continuum rather than two unrelated diatheses (Crow and Cooper 1986).

This conclusion is closely similar to that reached by Angst and co-workers (Angst et al. 1983) on the basis of their recent studies of the whole range of psychotic illness:

> The underlying hypothesis of a continuum of psychoses from depression to schizophrenia is not disproved by our results. They show that on a descriptive level of symptoms and syndromes, taking into account the whole course of a psychosis, the dichotomy into schizophrenic and affective psychoses is highly questionable. We do not only find transitional groups of schizoaffective patients but also marked affective symptomatology underlying or superimposed to schizophrenia. . . . Based on our findings we do not conclude that a unitary psychosis exists but we think of a continuum of psychopathological subgroups with a lot of overlap which may also differ to a certain extent in other respects such as course, genetics and response to treatment. (p. 259)

In a later analysis, Stassen et al. (1988) conclude:

> The principal goal of the present investigation has been to test the phenotypical equivalence of the two populations of index cases and their relatives . . . the results show that typical symptom patterns clearly appear in both populations. . . . Nevertheless our analyses revealed no clear breeding true of either affective disorders or schizophrenia. (p. 115)

The hypothesis of a continuum of psychosis is a development of the concept of the "unitary psychosis" espoused in the last century by Guislain (1833), Neumann (1859), and Griesinger (1861) and more recently by others (Flor-Henry 1983; Karlsson 1974; Llopis 1954; Menninger et al. 1958; Rennert 1982). A "spectrum" concept of the psychoses was also formulated by Beck (1972), who considered that two variables were involved: a schizophrenic variable linked to a poor prognosis and an affective variable linked to a good prognosis. According to the present concept, the psychoses are represented as a continuum from pure affective illness to deteriorating schizophrenia (Figure 1).

Ödegaard's (1963, 1972) conception of a "multifactorial" genetic background was based on observations of overlap in family studies in a series of consecutive admissions and is similar to that developed here. In Odegaard's 1972 chapter, the range of diagnosis in the proband was extended to include schizophrenic psychoses of three grades of defect, and the categories of schizophrenia without defect, reactive psychosis, and atypical affective psychosis probably cover most of what would be described as schizoaffective illness in other classifications. The incidence and types of illness in relatives are compatible with the concept of a continuum within which particular forms of illness are genetically related to those nearby. The interrelatedness of the two ends of the continuum, however, is limited. That movement along this continuum occurs is documented by Odegaard's study and the studies on schizoaffective disorder (e.g., those of Angst and colleagues); that such movements take place in the course of reproduction is suggested by the systematic trend in the intergenerational studies. For the children of parents with one type of psychosis, the risk of an illness of greater severity is increased. These phenomena cast some light on the nature of the underlying genetic mechanisms. They suggest that the gene responsible for typical affective disorder is closely related to, but not the same as, that underlying a deteriorating schizophrenic illness. The gene itself may be variable; the findings in parent-child pairs with psychosis suggest that such variations take place between generations (e.g., at meiosis), particularly in the direction of increasing severity. Therefore, one

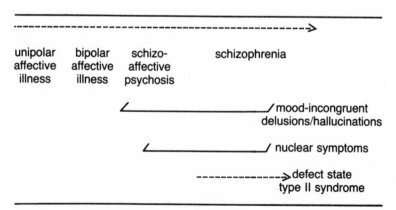

Figure 1.   The continuum concept. Brackets indicate the range over which mood-incongruent psychotic phenomena and nuclear symptoms may occur.

interpretation of the existence of a continuum is that the psychosis gene is associated with a high rate of mutation (Crow 1986).

CONCLUSION

Psychosis can be conceived as a continuum extending from unipolar through bipolar affective and schizoaffective disorders to schizophrenia with varying severities of defect. The continuum has a degree of stability in that relatives of probands at a particular point on the continuum are at risk of illnesses of a similar type, but there is also the possibility of change. Some evidence suggests change takes place between generations, perhaps particularly in the direction of increased severity. This concept is supported by three observations that challenge Kraepelin's binary view of the functional psychoses: 1) a bimodal distribution of the clinical features of manic-depressive illness and schizophrenia has not been demonstrated; 2) affective illness appears to predispose to schizophrenia in later generations; and 3) schizoaffective illnesses cannot be separated in family studies from either of the prototypical psychoses.

REFERENCES

American Psychiatric Association: Diagnostic and Statistical Manual of Mental Disorders, Third Edition. Washington, DC, American Psychiatric Association, 1980

Angst J, Felder W, Lohmeyer B: Schizoaffective disorders: I, results of a genetic investigation. J Affective Disord 1:139–153, 1979

Angst J, Scharfetter C, Stassen HH: Classification of schizo-affective patients by multidimensional scaling and cluster analysis. Psychiatria Clinica 16:254–264, 1983

Baron M, Gruen R, Asnis L, et al: Schizoaffective illness, schizophrenia and affective disorders. Acta Psychiatr Scand 65:253–262, 1982

Beck AT: Depression: Causes and Treatment. Philadelphia, University of Pennsylvania, 1972

Biederman J, Lerner Y, Belmaker RH: Combination of lithium carbonate and haloperidol in schizo-affective disorder. Arch Gen Psychiatry 36:327–333, 1979

Bland RC, Orn H: Schizophrenia: Schneider's first rank symptoms and outcome. Br J Psychiatry 137:63–68, 1980

Boklage CE: Schizophrenia, brain asymmetry development and twinning: cellular relationship with etiological and possibly prognostic implications. Biol Psychiatry 12:19–35, 1977

Brockington IF, Kendell RE, Wainwright S: Depressed patients with schizophrenia or paranoid symptoms. Psychol Med 10:665–675, 1980

Brown R, Colter N, Corsellis JAN, et al: Post-mortem evidence of structural brain changes in schizophrenia. Arch Gen Psychiatry 43:36–42, 1986

Clark JA, Mallett BL: A follow-up study of schizophrenia and depression in young adults. Br J Psychiatry 109:491–499, 1963

Cloninger CR, Martin RL, Guze SB, et al: Diagnosis and prognosis in schizophrenia. Arch Gen Psychiatry 42:15–25, 1985

Croughan JL, Welner A, Robins E: The group of schizo-affective and related psychoses—critique, record, follow-up and family studies. Arch Gen Psychiatry 31:632–637, 1974

Crow TJ: The continuum of psychosis and its implication for the structure of the gene. Br J Psychiatry 149:419–429, 1986

Crow TJ: Psychosis as a continuum and the virogene concept. Br Med Bull 43:754–767, 1987

Crow TJ, Cooper SJ: The genetics of the unitary psychosis, in Proceedings of the IVth World Congress of Biological Psychiatry. Edited by Shagass C, et al. Amsterdam, Elsevier, 1986

Davis JM: Overview: maintenance therapy in psychiatry: I, schizophrenia. Am J Psychiatry 132:1237–1245, 1975

Davis JM: Overview: maintenance therapy in psychiatry: II, affective disorders. Am J Psychiatry 133:1–13, 1976

Delva NJ, Letemendia FJJ: Lithium treatment in schizophrenia and schizoaffective disorders, in Contemporary Issues in Schizophrenia. Edited by Kerr A, Snaith RP. London, Gaskell, 1986

Elsasser G: Die Nachkommen Geisteskranker Elternpaare. Stuttgart, G Thieme, 1952

Feighner JP, Robins E, Guze SB, et al: Diagnostic criteria for use in psychiatric research. Arch Gen Psychiatry 26:57–63, 1972

Flor-Henry P: Cerebral Basis of Psychopathology. Bristol, J Wright, 1983

Gershon ES, Rieder RO: Are mania and schizophrenia genetically distinct? in Mania: An Evolving Concept. Edited by Belmaker RH, van Praag HM. New York, Spectrum, 1980

Gershon ES, Hamovit J, Guroff JJ, et al: A family study of schizo-affective, bipolar I, bipolar II, unipolar and normal control patients. Arch Gen Psychiatry 39:1157–1167, 1982

Gershon ES, DeLisi LE, Hamovit J, et al: A controlled family study of chronic psychoses. Arch Gen Psychiatry 45:328–336, 1988

Griesinger W: Die Pathologie und Therapie der Psychischen Krankheiten. Stuttgart, Krabbe, 1861

Guislain J: Traite des Phrenopathies. Brussels, Etablissement Encyclographique, 1833

Hollister LE, Overall JE, Shelton J, et al: Drug therapy of depression: amitriptyline, perphenazine and their combination in different syndromes. Arch Gen Psychiatry 17:486–493, 1967

Hunt RC, Appel KE: Prognosis in the psychoses lying midway between schizophrenia and manic-depressive psychoses. Am J Psychiatry 93:313–339, 1936

Johnstone EC, Crow TJ, Frith CD, et al: The Northwick Park "functional psychosis" study: diagnosis and treatment response. Lancet 2:119–125, 1988

Johnstone EC, Crow TJ, Frith CD, et al: Cerebral ventricular size and cognitive impairment in chronic schizophrenia. Lancet 2:924–926, 1976

Kant O: The incidence of psychoses and other mental abnormalities in the families of recovered and deteriorated schizophrenic patients. Psychiatr Q 16:176–186, 1942

Karlsson JL: The rate of schizophrenia in foster reared close relatives of schizophrenic index cases. Biol Psychiatry 2:285–290, 1970

Karlsson JL: Inheritance of schizophrenia. Acta Psychiatr Scand Suppl 274:1–116, 1974

Kasanin J: The acute schizo-affective psychoses. Am J Psychiatry 90:97–126, 1933

Kendell RE, Brockington IF: The identification of disease entities and the relationship between schizophrenia and affective psychoses. Br J Psychiatry 137:324–331, 1980

Kendell RE, Gourlay J: The clinical distinction between the affective psychoses and schizophrenia. Br J Psychiatry 117:261–266, 1970

Kendler KS, Hays P: Schizophrenia subdivided by the family history of affective disorder. Arch Gen Psychiatry 40:951–955, 1983

Kendler KS, Tsuang MT: Identical twins concordant for the progression of affective illness to schizophrenia. Br J Psychiatry 141:563–566, 1982

Kendler KS, Gruenberg AM, Tsuang MT: Psychiatric illness in the first degree relatives of schizophrenic and surgical control patients: a family study using DSM-III criteria. Arch Gen Psychiatry 42:770–779, 1985

Kraepelin E: Psychiatrie, 6th ed. Leipzig, Barth, 1899

Kraepelin E: Die Erscheinungsformen des Irreseins (1920), translated in Themes and Variations in European Psychiatry. Edited by Hirsch SR, Shepherd M. Bristol, J Wright, 1974, pp 7–30

Llopis B: La psicosis unica. Arch Neurobiol (Madr) 17:1–39, 1954

Loranger AW: Genetic independence of manic-depression and schizophrenia. Acta Psychiatr Scand 63:444–452, 1981

Magnan V: Leçons Clinique sur les Maladies Mentales. Paris, Battaile, 1893

McGue M, Gottesman II, Rao DC: The transmission of schizophrenia under a multifactorial threshold model. Am J Hum Genet 35:1161–1178, 1983

McGuffin P, Reveley AM, Holland A: Identical triplets: nonidentical psychosis? Br J Psychiatry 140:1–6, 1982

Menninger K, Ellenberger H, Pruyser P, et al: The unitary concept of mental illness. Bull Menninger Clin 22:4–12, 1958

Morel BA: Traité des Maladies Mentales. Paris, Masson, 1860

Myerson A: The Inheritance of Mental Diseases. Baltimore, Williams & Wilkins, 1925

Neumann H: Lehrbuch der Psychiatrie. Erlangen, F Enke, 1859

Odegaard O: The psychiatric disease entities in the light of a genetic investigation. Acta Psychiatrica et Neurologica Scandinavica 39:94–104, 1963

Odegaard O: The multifactorial inheritance of predisposition to schizophrenia, in Genetic Factors in "Schizophrenia." Edited by Kaplan AR. Springfield, Ill, Charles C Thomas, 1972

Penrose LS: Critical survey of schizophrenia genetics, in Modern Perspectives in World Psychiatry. Edited by Howells JG. Edinburgh, Oliver and Boyd, 1968

Pollock HM, Malzberg B: Hereditary and environmental factors in the causation of manic-depressive psychoses and dementia praecox. Am J Psychiatry 96:1227–1247, 1940

Pope HG, Lipinski JF: Diagnosis in schizophrenia and manic-depressive illness: a reassessment of the specificity of "schizophrenic" symptoms in the light of current research. Arch Gen Psychiatry 35:811–828, 1978

Powell A, Thomson N, Hall DJ, et al: Parent-child concordance with respect to sex and diagnosis in schizophrenia and manic-depressive psychosis. Br J Psychiatry 123:653–658, 1973

Pulver AE, Stewart W, Carpenter WT, et al: Risk factors in schizophrenia: season of birth in Maryland, U.S.A. Br J Psychiatry 143:389–396, 1983

Rao DC, Morton NE, Gottesman II, et al: Path analysis of qualitative data on pairs of relatives. Hum Hered 31:325–333, 1981

Reich T, Cloninger CR, Suarez B, et al: Genetics of the affective disorders, in Handbook of Psychiatry, Vol 3, Psychoses of Uncertain Aetiology. Edited by Wing JK, Wing L. Cambridge, Cambridge University Press, 1982

Rennert H: Zum Modell "Universalgenese der Psychosen"—Aspekte einer unkonventionellen Auffasung der psychische Krankheiten. Fortschr Neurol Psychiatr 50:1–29, 1982

Rosenthal D: Genetic Theory and Abnormal Behaviour. New York, McGraw-Hill, 1970

Schneider K: Primare and sekundare Symptoms bei der Schizophrenie. Fortschr Neurol Psychiatr 25:487–490, 1957

Schulz B: Kinder manische-depressiver und anderer affectiv psychotischer Elternpaare. Zeitschrift fur die Gesamte Neurologie und Psychiatrie 169:311–412, 1940

Sheldrick C: The validity of the distinction between schizophrenia and manic-depressive psychosis. M Phil. thesis. University of London, 1975

Sheldrick C, Jablensky A, Sartorius N, et al: Schizophrenia succeeded by affective illness: catamnestic study and statistical enquiry. Psychol Med 7:619–624, 1977

Slater E: Inheritance of manic-depressive insanity. Lancet 1:429–431, 1936

Slater E: Psychotic and Neurotic Illness in Twins. Medical Research Council Special Report series no. 278. London, Her Majesty's Stationery Office, 1953

Stassen HH, Scharfetter CH, Winokur G, et al: Familial syndrome patterns in schizophrenia, schizo-affective disorder, mania and depression. Eur Arch Psychiatr Neurol Sci 237:115–123, 1988

Tsuang MT: Schizo-affective disorder: dead or alive? Arch Gen Psychiatry 36:633–634, 1979

Tsuang MT, Dempsey GM, Dvoredsky N, et al: A family history study of schizo-affective disorder. Biol Psychiatry 12:331–338, 1977

Tsuang MT, Winokur G, Crowe RR: Morbidity risks of schizophrenia and affective disorders among first degree relatives of patients with schizophrenia, mania, depression and surgical conditions. Br J Psychiatry 137:497–504, 1980

Watson GC, Kucala T, Angulski G, et al: Season of birth and schizophrenia: a response to the Lewis and Griffin critique. J Abnorm Psychol 91:120–125, 1982

Chapter 6

Genetic Marker Studies in Schizophrenia and Affective Disorder: Is There Biological Evidence for a Continuum of the Clinical Syndromes?

Lynn E. DeLisi, M.D.
Anne L. Hoff, Ph.D.

Chapter 6

Genetic Marker Studies in Schizophrenia and Affective Disorder: Is There Biological Evidence for a Continuum of the Clinical Syndromes?

EVIDENCE FOR A GENETIC CAUSE FOR PSYCHOSIS

In discussions of the etiology of dementia praecox, Kraepelin (1907) wrote that "defective heredity is a very prominent factor . . . and appears in about 70 percent of cases." About bipolar disorder, he concluded that "hereditary taint" could be demonstrated in about 80% of cases observed in Heidelberg (Kraepelin 1921). These, of course, were conclusions drawn from his personal clinical experience and not a systematic survey of families. Since his time and the beginnings of attempts of others to distingush bipolar disorder from schizophrenia, several family, twin, and adoption studies have established a genetic influence on the development of both schizophrenia and affective disorder (reviewed by Gershon et al. 1988; Gottesman and Shields 1982). It is controversial, however, whether the morbid risk for affective disorder is elevated among first-degree relatives of probands with schizophrenia; and whether the risk for schizophrenia is elevated among first-degree relatives of probands with affective disorder (Tables 1 and 2). Further confusion exists when first-degree relatives of probands with schizoaffective disorder are examined (Table 3). These individuals have an increased risk for both schizophrenia and affective disorder among first-degree relatives. See Rogers and Winokur (Chapter 4) and Crow (Chapter 5) for further evidence from family studies for and against a continuum of the clinical syndromes of affective disorder and schizophrenia.

101

The schizophrenia family studies can probably be divided into the older European—or pre-DSM-III (American Psychiatric Association 1980) era—studies and the few American surveys published after 1980. In a summary of the pooled European family data, Gottesman and Shields (1982) estimated the risk to relatives of schizophrenic probands for schizophrenia to be 10.1% in siblings, 5.6% in parents, and 12.8% in children. The risk to second-degree relatives varies from 2.4% to 4.2%. The risk to third-degree relatives is approximately 2.4%.

Morbid risks from affective disorder family studies vary with proband diagnosis. For bipolar I probands, the risk of illness in first-degree relatives is 4.5% for bipolar I illness, 4.1% for bipolar II illness, 14% for unipolar illness, and 1.1% for schizoaffective illness (Gershon et al. 1982). Results from this same study show risks of

Table 1. Prevalence of Schizophrenia in First-Degree Relatives of Probands with Affective Disorder

Reference	Proband diagnosis	Diagnosis in first-degree relatives	
		Schizophrenia	Schizoaffective disorder
Angst et al. (1980)	Bipolar	1.9	1.5
	Unipolar	1.2	.9
Tsuang et al. (1980)	Mania	*3.2	
	Depression	1.7	
	Control	.6	
Gershon et al. (1982)	Bipolar I	.2	1.1
	Bipolar II	.5	.6
	Unipolar	0	.7
	Control	0	.5
Baron et al. (1982)	SA-A	0	*3.2 (SA-A)
	Bipolar	.7	1.5 (SA-A)
	Unipolar	0	*3.0 (SA-A)
			.8 (SA-S)
	Schizophrenia	7.9	1.7 (SA-S)
Weissman et al. (1984)	Unipolar (severe)	.4	.8
	Unipolar (mild)	.2	0
	Control	.2	.2

Note. SA-A = schizoaffective, mainly affective; SA-S = schizoaffective, mainly schizophrenic. * $p < .05$ (increased from control population).

illness in families of unipolar probands as 1.5% for bipolar I illness, 1.5% for bipolar II illness, 16.6% for unipolar illness, and .7% for schizoaffective illness. Lifetime prevalences of major affective disorder are 37%, 24%, 25%, 20%, and 7% for relatives of probands with schizoaffective illness, bipolar I illness, bipolar II illness, unipolar illness, and normal controls, respectively. Morbid risk to offspring is 74% when two parents are ill and 27% when one parent is ill. Based on these data, the authors proposed a continuum of genetic vulnerability, with greater severity associated with expression of bipolar illness and less vulnerability predisposing to unipolar illness. Other family studies of affective disorder vary from these data in absolute percentages, but consistently show that rates are elevated over controls.

The risks for schizophrenia are generally equal for male and female relatives, although in general the morbid risk to female relatives for all affective disorder is significantly greater than for male relatives. Pairs of first-degree relatives with psychosis are more likely to be the same sex than opposite sex; parent-child pairs are more likely to be mother-child than father-child; and sibling pairs are more likely to be the same sex than opposite sex (reviewed by Crow 1988; Ro-

Table 2. Prevalence of Affective Disorder in First-Degree Relatives of Probands with Schizophrenia

Reference	Proband diagnosis	Diagnosis in first-degree relative		
		Bipolar I	Unipolar	Schizoaffective
Tsuang et al. (1980)	Schizophrenia	*1.9	5.9	
	Control	.2	4.8	
Guze et al. (1983)	Schizophrenia (+ Schizoaffective)	0	2.7	
	?Schizophrenia	0	8.1	
	Other	1.1	5.7	
Baron et al. (1985)	Schizophrenia	.3	5.2	
	Control	0	3.3	
Kendler et al. (1985)	Schizophrenia	1.3	6.0	*1.4
	Control	.3	7.6	.1
Gershon et al. (1988)	Schizophrenia	*1.3	*14.7	
	Schizoaffective	*8.8	*9.3	*5.0
	Control	.3	6.7	.6

$*p < .05.$

Table 3. Prevalence of Schizophrenia and Affective Disorder in First-Degree Relatives of Probands with Schizoaffective Disorder

Reference	Proband diagnosis	Diagnosis in first-degree relative				
		Schizophrenia	Bipolar I	Bipolar II	Unipolar	Schizoaffective
Gershon et al. (1982)	Schizoaffective	3.6	10.7	6.1	14.5	6.1
	Normal Control	0	0	.5	5.8	.5
Angst et al. (1979)	Schizoaffective	5.3	1.1		5.6	3.0
Mendlewicz et al. (1980)	Schizoaffective	10.8	34.6(all)			
	Schizophrenia	16.9	8.6			
	Unipolar	3.2	28.5			
	Bipolar	1.8	39.4			
Baron et al. (1982)	SA-A	0	1.6		26.5	3.2
	SA-S	4.1	0		10.9	1.4

Note. SA-A = schizoaffective, mainly affective; SA-S = schizoaffective, mainly schizophrenic.

senthal 1962). In addition, there is some indication that relatives of female probands may be at greater risk for schizophrenia than the relatives of male probands (Macciardi et al., 1987; Tsuang et al. unpublished observations). All the above risks are significantly higher than would be expected in the unrelated general population (.1% to 1%), although these studies have generally not surveyed a specific control group for comparison. The more recent American studies are separately notable for their more structured diagnostic design and use of carefully examined controls. Taken together, these also define a significant excess of schizophrenia in first-degree relatives of schizophrenic probands using DSM-III criteria, ranging to approximately 8% (Baron et al. 1985; Gershon et al. 1988; Guze et al. 1983; Tsuang et al. 1980).

There are approximately 12 major studies of schizophrenic twin pairs comparing monozygotic (MZ) with same-sex dizygotic (DZ) concordance rates. While these rates also vary from study to study, it is clear that significantly higher concordance rates are found among MZ twins compared with DZ twins in all studies—an overall concordance rate of 50% for MZ twins and 18% for DZ twins, summarized in Gottesman and Shields (1982) (see Table 3). Similarly, there are at least seven major twin studies of affective disorder that demonstrate greater concordance for illness in MZ twins as compared to DZ twins—a pooled concordance rate of 69% for MZ twins versus 13% for DZ twins, reviewed in Gershon et al. (1976) (see Table 4). Using the Danish Twin Register, Bertelsen and colleagues

Table 4. Twin Concordance Rates and Morbid Risk to First-Degree Relatives, in Percentages

	Schizophrenia	Affective disorder		
		Bipolar	Unipolar	All
Twin concordance rates				
Monozygotic	50	79	54	69
Dizygotic	18	24	19	13
Morbid risk to first-degree relatives	5.6–12.8	8.6[a]	14	(up to) 31.9

Note. Twin concordance rates for schizophrenia adapted from Gottesman and Shields (1982). Pooled affective disorder data from Gershon et al. (1976, 1982). Bipolar and unipolar twin data from Bertelsen (1979) and Bertelsen et al. (1977).
[a]Bipolar I and II.

found pairwise concordance was 79% in bipolar MZ twins versus 54% in unipolar MZ twins, whereas DZ concordance rates were comparable at 24% and 19%, respectively, for both illnesses (Bertelsen 1979; Bertelsen et al. 1977). Of the 110 pairs studied, 7 were mixed with regard to polarity (unipolar or bipolar), suggesting possible overlap in genetic vulnerability between the subtypes of affective disorder. Proponents of environmental causes for psychoses, however, will emphasize that in no study does the MZ concordance rate reach 100%.

Using twin concordance rates or family study data, several investigators have calculated the heritability, or extent to which the variance in liability is due to genetic factors, to be between 60% and 70% for schizophrenia (Carter and Chung 1980; Kendler 1983; McGue et al. 1983, 1985; Rao et al. 1981; Risch and Baron 1984). Although similar calculations are not found in the literature for affective disorder, they are presumed to be at least as high, based on the overall MZ-DZ differences (Table 3). To distinguish the relative importance of the genetic versus environmental component to the development of schizophrenia, Rosenthal and Kety embarked on a landmark series of studies that all strongly suggest that children removed from biological parents at birth are still significantly at greater risk for schizophrenia if there is schizophrenia among their biological relatives, but not their adoptive relatives (Kety et al. 1975; Rosenthal et al. 1971). A more recent adoption study completed in Finland has also independently confirmed this finding (Tienari et al. 1985). Similar adoption studies of affective disorder probands also suggest a higher proportion of illness among biological relatives than nonbiological relatives or control families, although the data are more equivocal. Studying 29 bipolar adoptees, Mendlewicz and Rainer (1977) found affective disorder in 31% of biological parents versus 2% of biological and 9% of adoptive parents of normal adoptees. Kety (1979) and Schulsinger et al. (1979) also found an excess of suicides among the biological relatives of adoptees with affective disorder. Although one Swedish adoption study (Von Knorring et al. 1983) failed to confirm these findings, the ill adoptees were predominantly unipolar depressed and nonpsychotic; thus genetic influences may be less in these subtypes of illness. Indeed, Torgersen's (1986) data from a Norwegian twin study do not support the role of genetic influences in dysthymia, adjustment disorder with depression, and nonpsychotic major depression. The phenotypic variability seen in unipolar and bipolar depressive disorders as well as evidence for nongenetic factors accounting for certain familial patterns in depression make genetic studies of affective disorder more problematic. While there is stronger evidence for genetic transmissability of bipolar disorder than unipolar, their genetic relationship needs further investigation. Reich et al. (1986) found some evidence for genetic independence among bipolar and unipolar diagnoses, whereas Gershon et al. (1976) and others (e.g., Clayton 1986) have provided data that support a continuity, with bipolar at one extreme and nonrecurrent unipolar depression at the other.

Another piece of evidence against an environmental cause for at least the onset of psychosis comes from the series of studies examining the age of onset of illness in pairs of siblings. In a review of this literature, Crow and Done (1986) combined all studied pairs and calculated whether onset of illness in one member of a pair influenced the time of onset in the second. They found, however, that age of onset among siblings was significantly correlated, whereas the actual time of onset was not, suggesting a prenatal determination, possibly genetic, of the timing of onset of illness within families and no significant postnatal effect. Age of onset in pairs of siblings with affective disorder has not been specifically studied, although some of the pairs in the above-mentioned series of studies would most likely satisfy present structured criteria for affective psychoses.

Finally, while rarer than the family prevalence statistics may suggest, occasionally families are found with clusters of members with schizophrenia and affective disorder spanning multiple generations, and some having both illnesses within the same family. It is difficult to determine whether, in the latter instance, two independent genetic mechanisms are involved or whether the genetics of both are related. Given that both schizophrenia and bipolar disorder are present in less than 1% of the general population, it is unlikely that this could happen by chance and implies that genetic transmission must be occurring. Unipolar depression, on the other hand, is far more prevalent; thus when present in multiple generations, the genetics may become more complex.

THE MODE OF INHERITANCE

Despite numerous clinical studies based on large populations, a specific pattern of inheritance has not been established for either disorder, and the literature in this area remains inconsistent. Using morbid risk figures, or segregation analysis, several mechanisms have been proposed. The genetic component (or components) of liability can be modeled either as a single major locus or as a large number of genes, each with small additive effects (polygenic). One model of transmission assumes a combination of a number of underlying genetic and environmental liability factors such that a person who reaches a quantitative threshold of these factors develops the illness. Single locus and polygenic inheritance can be differentiated on the basis that they predict different patterns of inheritance of illness in relatives of patients and can be modeled mathematically. Thus Rao et al. (1981), using morbid risk figures from summed European family study data, showed that a multifactorial threshold model would be the most likely explanation for transmission of schizophrenia. Other studies using segregation analysis, which take into account pedigree structure, however, are contradictory. Some provide evidence for dominant single major locus transmission; others are consistent with polygenes (Carter and Chung 1980). In one, the investigators concluded that pure polygenic transmission could not be distinguished from a major recessive locus with a polygenic component (Risch and Baron 1984). Most segregation analyses of families with affective disorders provide evidence against single major locus transmission (Bucher and Elston 1981; Bucher et al. 1981; Crowe et al. 1981; Goldin et al. 1983; Tsuang et al. 1985), and generally are consistent with a polygenic mode of inheritance (Gershon et al. 1975, 1982; Smeraldi et al. 1981). While, taken together, these analyses for both disorders appear to suggest polygenic transmission, most do not rule out that a single major locus could be responsible for either illness in at least some families.

All these models have been limited in their power to identify a clear mode of transmission for several reasons. First, particularly with respect to schizophrenia, many of the family studies on which analyses are based have relied on family history diagnoses that may not meet present criteria for the disorder and have also not been sensitive to the broader spectrum of related personality disorders. With respect to segregation analyses for both illnesses, the models have not considered that the extent of the clinical boundaries may be even broader than those used, and have not included both the spectrum of schizophrenic-like illness and affective disorder in the same sets of analyses (Crow 1984). A recent clinical family study of schizophrenia completed at the National Institute of Mental Health (NIMH) suggests that there may be considerable genetic overlap between schizophrenia and affective disorder (Gershon et al. 1988). As can be seen by the reviews in Rogers and Winokur (Chapter 4, this volume) and Crow (Chapter 5, this volume), however, this issue is quite debatable.

Second, the analyses to date have not considered the role played by unknown environmental variables in the expression of the disorder, and do not deal adequately with incomplete gene penetrance. Stimulation studies have shown that a single major locus is often not detectable by segregation analysis when the heterozygote penetrance is low (5% to 20%) or when there are substantial numbers of nongenetic phenocopies in the population. However, under these conditions, a major locus can be detected if there is a closely linked marker locus (Goldin et al. 1981, 1984).

Third, and perhaps most important, the above inconsistencies may have resulted from considering both categories of disorders (schizophrenia and affective disorder) as single (as well as separate) etiologic entities. It is possible that significant subgroups may emerge with different but clear patterns of inheritance and that, at least in these subgroups, major psychiatric disability may be caused by one or more major genetic loci.

Finally, a number of further methodological limitations are also apparent, particularly in genetic studies of affective disorder. The heterogeneity of symptom presentation, including such diagnostically diverse syndromes as alcohol use, adjustment disorder, dysthymia, and unipolar and bipolar disorders, makes the calculation of genetic models overly complex. As summarized by Blehar et al. (1988), the issues of a possible cohort effect and of diagnostic stability over time must be addressed in the genetic studies of affective disorder. Similar to studies of alcoholism, bipolar disorder, and suicide, Klerman et al. (1985) found an increase in the prevalence rates of major depression in each separate birth cohort beginning from World War II, implying a major environmental effect on the prevalence of mood disorders.

Thus, given the above limitations in our research designs and the fact that no inherited biological factor has been found to be consistently abnormal in either patients with schizophrenia or affective disorder and segregate with illness within high-density families (reviewed in DeLisi et al. 1987a; Erlenmeyer-Kimling 1987; Gershon et al. 1987), it is not surprising that, at present, there are no obvious clues for determining what is inherited and which gene is the most likely one to pursue. The following is a review of the major biological and direct genetic markers that have been examined to date, noting the similarity of findings in both disorders.

BIOLOGICAL MARKER STUDIES

Over the last few decades, numerous studies have been published comparing samples of unrelated patients with control groups quantifying different biochemical substances in urine, plasma, cerebrospinal fluid (CSF), and postmortem brain (reviewed in DeLisi and Wyatt 1985). Interpretation of these studies has been complicated by the unclear influences of environmental variables, even though some abnormalities have been consistently replicated in several independent populations. What is remarkable, however, is that no biological marker, when studied in patients with both affective disorder and schizophrenia, has been found to be unique to one or the other illness. The following are examples of putative biological markers that have at one time been extensively studied in patients with these disorders (see Table 5).

Monoamine Oxidase

The most extensively studied substance in schizophrenic patients, an enzyme of major importance in monoamine metabolism, is monoamine oxidase (MAO). The B form of the enzyme is easily assayed in platelets and thought to be representative of the B form in the human brain. The hypothesis that abnormalities in MAO may be associated with schizophrenia is supported by the known major role of MAO in the metabolism of dopamine. Low MAO activity could explain elevated dopaminergic activity and would be consistent with the dopamine hypothesis of schizophrenia. Numerous studies of platelet MAO activity in the 1970s resulted in reports of reduced activity of this enzyme in populations of chronic schizophrenic patients, in individuals with other major psychiatric disease, as well as in patients with miscellaneous other conditions (reviewed by DeLisi et al. 1982). In affective disorders, most investigators also found decreased platelet MAO in patients with bipolar illness (Gershon et al. 1977). However, high platelet MAO has also been reported in depressed patients, and these patients have a preponderance of rel-

Table 5. Biological Markers in Schizophrenia and Affective Disorder

	Schizophrenia	Affective disorder
Monoamine metabolism		
MAO activity	Reduced	Reduced
Homovanillic acid	Decreased in CSF in subgroup with brain atrophy	Decreased in CSF in depression
MHPG	No difference	Decreased
Norepinephrine	Increased	Unknown
Phenylethylamine	Increased	Increased
Serotonin	Increased	Unknown
5-HIAA	1 study decreased in CSF in subgroup with brain atrophy	Decreased 5-HIAA associated with suicide attempts

Table 5. Biological Markers in Schizophrenia and Affective Disorder—Continued

	Schizophrenia	Affective disorder
Receptors		
Dopamine	Increased	Unknown
Alpha-2 adrenergic	Increased	Increased
Beta-adrenergic	Unknown	Increased
Cholinergic activity	REM latency decreased?	REM latency decreased
Membrane transport		
Lithium transport	Unknown	Abnormal
Phospholipid ratios	Abnormal	Unknown
Brain morphology		
Lateral ventricular size	Increased	Increased
Temporal lobe size	Increased	Increased
3rd ventricle size	Increased	Unknown
Smooth pursuit eye movement	Abnormal	Abnormal
Chromosomal abnormalities	Increased XXY	Increased XXY
RFLP linkages		
Chromosome 5q	1 positive study	(includes affective disorder)
Chromosome 11p	Not found	1 positive study
Sex chromosome Xq	Not found	2 positive studies (1 non-RFLP marker)

Note. Summary of the majority of studies. The significance of these differences between patients and controls has generally not been established. Several of these findings (i.e., p-MAO reductions) may be an artifact of neuroleptic treatment. All these findings are present in subgroups, not all, of the patients. Some of these subgroups have been associated with specific clinical symptoms. MAO = monoamine oxidase; MHPG = 3-methoxy-4-hydroxyphenylethylene glycol; 5-HIAA = 5-hydroxyindoleacetic acid; CSF = cerebrospinal fluid; REM = rapid eye movement; RFLP = restriction fragment length polymorphisms.

atives with bipolar illness; patients with low platelet MAO tend to have increased prevalence of alcoholism and neurotic depression in their families (Von Knorring et al. 1985). While MAO activity in the brains of suicide victims appears similar to that of normal controls

(Grote et al. 1974; Mann and Stanley 1984), alcoholic patients who commit suicide appear to have lower MAO activity (Gottfries et al. 1975). These findings are consistent with other studies that demonstrate low platelet MAO activity in alcoholics as a whole (e.g., Oreland et al. 1984).

The level of MAO activity was found to be highly heritable and to have a pattern of inheritance consistent with X linkage (Nies et al. 1971). Two studies of MZ twins discordant for schizophrenia showed lower platelet MAO activity in twins with one schizophrenic member than in control twin pairs, although the ill twins tend to have lower enzyme activity than their well co-twins despite having identical genes (Reveley et al. 1983; Wyatt et al. 1973). This work, while interpreted as an indication for a genetic vulnerability toward decreased MAO activity in schizophrenia, also suggests an environmental effect on enzyme activity. Further family studies of MAO activity have generally not found an association of low activity with illness within families (DeLisi et al. 1980; Rice et al. 1984). Neuroleptics were subsequently found to lower platelet MAO activity to the degree seen in populations of patients (DeLisi et al. 1981b; Owen et al. 1981), and thus interest was lost in the utility of this measurement as a biological marker of illness.

Examples also exist of other enzymes crucial to monoamine metabolism that have been examined in tissue studies, but for which significant differences have generally not emerged. These enzymes include dopamine-beta-hydroxylase and catecholamine-O-methyl transferase, both of which have also been found to have highly heritable measurable peripheral activity (Weinshilbaum and Raymond 1977; Weinshilbaum et al. 1975). Although peripheral enzymes themselves may no longer be valid markers for studying brain metabolism, newer approaches focusing directly on genes for these enzymes may be warranted.

Monoamines and Their Metabolites

The metabolites of monoamine neurotransmitters (dopamine, norepinephrine, and serotonin) have been studied extensively in both disorders. Some studies of 5-hydroxyindoleacetic acid (5-HIAA) levels in CSF suggest significantly lower levels in depressed patients (Agren 1980; Asberg et al. 1984); others show no differences between unmedicated patients and controls (Banki et al. 1981a; Roy et al. 1985). Subgroups of chronic schizophrenic patients have also been reported to have significantly lower CSF 5-HIAA levels (Potkin et al. 1983) and elevated blood serotonin (DeLisi et al. 1981a). Sedvall and colleagues (Sedvall and Wode-Helgodt 1980; Sedvall et al. 1980) determined CSF 5-HIAA levels using the family history dichotomy for detection of inheritance of differences in the metabolism of these transmitters as markers for illness. Family-history-positive schizophrenic patients were found to have higher CSF 5-HIAA and homovanillic acid (HVA) levels than family-history-negative patients, indicating increased turnover of both dopamine and serotonin in the familial subgroup of patients. On the other hand, depressed patients with a family history of depression were found to have lower CSF 5-HIAA levels than family-history-negative patients. Similarly, normal individuals with a positive family history for depression had lower CSF 5-HIAA levels than those with a negative family history. Normal individuals with a family history of psychosis tended to have higher CSF 5-HIAA and HVA levels than those with negative family histories, although the numbers of individuals in these studies are small. The same investigators also examined the heritability of these markers using MZ and DZ comparisons (Oxenstierna et al. 1986). Although a familial influence was found for both HVA and 5-HIAA, cultural heritability (familial environment) appeared larger than the genetic effect.

Van Praag and de Hann (1979) also found an increased incidence of depression in the families of depressed patients with low CSF 5-HIAA levels compared to patients with normal levels. Although the data are not clear, it may be that 5-HIAA levels are related to aspects of depression (e.g., suicide potential) regardless of actual diagnosis. For example, among suicide attempters, patients with low 5-HIAA levels were 10 times more likely to succeed in committing suicide than the rest of the group (Traskman et al. 1981).

Similarly, the literature on HVA reveals some studies finding lower HVA levels in the CSF of depressed patients (Banki et al. 1981b; Berger et al. 1980) and others suggesting elevated levels in patient groups (Sweeney et al. 1978). Elevated levels may be associated with the presence of psychosis, particularly delusions (Aberg-Wistedt et al. 1985).

The CSF and plasma studies of schizophrenic patients appear the opposite. While low CSF HVA levels have been associated with a subgroup of chronic-defect-state patients, elevated plasma levels at baseline and significant declines with medication have been associated with pharmacological responsiveness—particularly with respect to psychotic symptoms (reviewed by Losonczy et al. 1987). Further studies to determine whether altered catecholamine or indolamine metabolism is related to the genetics of either disorder, and thus whether these can be useful as biological markers of illness, have not been done.

Norepinephrine metabolites, particularly 3-methoxy-4-hydroxy-phenylethylene glycol (MHPG), have been studied in affective disorder. In general, decreased 24-hour urinary excretion of MHPG has been reported in depressed patients, with particularly low concentrations seen in bipolar depressed individuals (Post et al. 1984; Rees et al. 1970). Urinary excretion of MHPG metabolites also appears to be state dependent, with higher levels noted in manic states (Pickar et al. 1978). The NIMH multicenter study, however, found no differences between depressed patients, both unipolar and bipolar, and normals in urinary MHPG secretion (Koslow et al. 1983). Studies of plasma MHPG parallel earlier urinary findings, with some variability noted in unipolar depression. High values have been seen in manic and some unipolar patients, and low values appear to be more likely in bipolar depressed patients (Post et al. 1984). In studies of schizophrenic patients, no differences have been reported between patient groups and normals in either urinary excretion of MHPG (DeLisi et al. 1983) or plasma concentrations (Ko et al. 1985).

Dopamine Receptors

An increased amount of functionally available dopamine receptors may also be another important marker of both schizophrenic and affective psychoses. Previous evidence from postmortem studies finding significantly increased D-2 dopamine receptors in the striatum of schizophrenic patients has been controversial due to the unclear influence of chronic neuroleptic treatment on dopamine receptor numbers (Crow and Johnstone 1987). The more recent in vivo positron emission tomography (PET) spiperone-binding studies, unfortunately, have only added to the controversy (Farde et al. 1987; Wong et al. 1986). The peripheral lymphocyte spiperone-binding results of Bondy and Ackenheil (1987), while confirming some of the positive postmortem studies and further demonstrating a familial aggregation of increased binding, have remained unreplicated, although several unpublished attempts have been made. Little has been done to examine dopamine receptor function in patients with affective disorder.

Adrenergic Receptors

Both the alpha-2 and beta adrenergic receptors have been studied as illness "markers" in peripheral blood systems of both patients with affective disorder and those with schizophrenia. Overall, the data are conflicting. While the density of these receptors on peripheral membranes is partially under genetic control, there are no family data available to suggest an association of abnormal receptor numbers with illness within families (reviewed by Gershon et al. 1987; Van Kammen and Gelernter 1987).

Cholinergic Receptor Response

The initiation of rapid eye movement (REM) sleep appears to be under muscarinic cholinergic control. Thus sensitivity to REM induction has been examined in affectively disordered patients as a means of understanding the role of the cholinergic nervous system in depression. Sitaram and colleagues (Nurnberger et al. 1983; Sitaram et al. 1980, 1984) have found that affectively disordered patients are more sensitive than normals to REM induction; that REM induction times are correlated among normal MZ twins; and that sensitivity to REM induction covaries with affective illness in relatives of patients with REM induction sensitivity. In schizophrenia, reports of the amount of REM sleep in schizophrenic patients varies, with some studies showing increased REM sleep (Gulavich et al. 1967) and others decreased REM sleep (Azumi 1966). REM latency in schizophrenia has also been variable, reported in one study to be reduced (Dement 1955) and in another normal (Feinberg et al. 1964). A more recent study by Zarcone et al. (1987) indicated that REM latencies of patients with schizophrenia, those with major depressive disorder, and those with schizoaffective disorder were indistinguishable.

It has also been reported that affectively disordered patients and their relatives have increased numbers of muscarinic receptor-binding sites compared with normals (Nadi et al. 1984), and that patients who committed suicide had greater muscarinic-binding activity in frontal regions of the brain than matched controls (Meyerson et al. 1982). However, these findings have not been replicated (Kaufman et al. 1984; Nadi et al. unpublished data). No studies have been reported of muscarinic receptors in schizophrenia.

Dexamethasone Suppression

While widely held at one time as a marker for endogenous depression, the lack of cortical response to dexamethasone challenge has also been found in patients with schizophrenia, as well as in patients with other miscellaneous disorders (reviewed by Arana and Baldessarini 1987). Whether this could be a useful marker of genetic vulnerability for any psychiatric disorder is doubtful.

Membrane Abnormalities

Red cell lithium transport has been studied in affective disorder and has been considered a marker of membrane transport function. While this mechanism appears to be under genetic control (Dorus et al. 1980), it has thus far not been shown to be related to the genetics of affective disorder (Waters et al. 1983) and has not been studied in family studies of schizophrenia.

Although controversial, membrane lipid pathology has long been reported in schizophrenia (reviewed in Rotrosen and Wolkin 1987). It is unknown whether a genetic component to psychiatric vulnerability could be related to a membrane structural difference (e.g., change in phospholipid content) because family studies of these abnormalities have not been done. The findings have also focused on schizophrenia; affective disorder has not been well examined.

Brain Morphological Abnormalities

Subtle brain morphological abnormalities (often of inherited origin) can be an early marker of illness in some patients, although it has not yet been clearly shown that they precede, rather than result from, the chronic deterioration characteristic of the illness. Despite the apparent demonstrated heritability of variations in brain ventricular size (DeLisi et al. 1986; Reveley et al. 1982), additional nongenetic factors also appear to contribute to the ventricular enlargement associated with schizophrenia (DeLisi et al. 1986; Reveley et al. 1984). While family studies of brain abnormalities have not been done in affective disorder, other studies clearly indicate that enlarged ventricles are also present in unrelated patients with affective disorder (Nasrallah et al. 1984; Pearlson et al. 1984; Targum et al. 1983), and present in a variety of other neuropsychiatric disorders as well.

Bilateral temporal lobe tissue reduction has also recently been found on magnetic resonance imaging (MRI) scans of both chronic patients with schizophrenia (DeLisi et al. 1988c; Johnstone et al. submitted; Weinberger 1988) and chronic patients with affective disorder (Hauser 1988).

Deviant Eye Tracking

While physiological traits appear the most removed from the basic defect, they may also serve as easily measurable markers of an illness if consistently present. The most interesting trait associated with schizophrenia is the presence of deviant smooth pursuit eye movements (SPEM), or "tracking" (the ability of the eye to follow a moving target). More than 60% of schizophrenics have been found in several studies to have abnormal SPEM (Holzman 1985; Lipton et al. 1983). This trait has also been shown to be heritable in twin and family studies and to be unaffected by neuroleptic medication (Holzman et al. 1974, 1980). The family studies of schizophrenic probands, however, do not show that abnormal SPEM segregates with schizophrenic illness, and schizophrenics with normal eye tracking are found to have well relatives with abnormal tracking. Nevertheless, abnormal SPEM has been found in excess among well first-degree relatives of schizophrenic, but not bipolar, patients. Although patients with bipolar illness also are found to have abnormal SPEM, these investigators suggested that it may be a state phenomenon related to lithium treatment. To provide an explanation for these findings, Matthysse et al. (1986) speculated that the gene (or genes) involved with genetic vulnerability for psychosis are expressed in variable ways; while some individuals with these genes may develop a psychosis, others may have only the presence of abnormal eye tracking. Perhaps the delineation of the mechanism for abnormal eye tracking will clarify the significance of these findings.

GENETIC MARKER STUDIES

Prior to the advent of techniques to identify DNA sequences for mapping chromosomes directly and tracing the genes for inherited diseases, protein polymorphisms were the only direct genetic markers available. These primarily consisted of blood group antigens and human leukocyte antigens (HLA) because of their highly variable expression. They were used to detect higher frequencies of specific variants occurring in association with a specific disorder (association studies), or to "mark" the inherited pattern to a specific gene, and those portions of the same chromosome closely linked to it within families (linkage studies). Linkage of the HLA region on chromosome 6 to schizophrenia was reported by Turner (1979), but subsequently rejected in two other more recent independent studies that were, unlike the Turner study, based on systematic diagnoses of family members (Goldin et al. 1987; McGuffin et al. 1983). Linkage of the HLA region to affective disorder originally reported by Weitkamp et al. (1981) has also been disconfirmed by others (Goldin et al. 1982; Targum et al. 1979).

ABO blood types have been studied in patients with schizophrenia and affective disorder; no consistent deviations from normal control distributions were noted (Goldin and Gershon 1983). While some investigators have found various blood types to be associated with subgroups of these disorders, most of these results can likely be accounted for by geographic skewness in patient population samples (Flemenbaum and Larson 1976). Many studies finding significant associations have been reported of one particular HLA type to paranoid and other subtypes of illness, but no HLA type has consistently been associated with schizophrenia or affective disorder (Goldin and Gershon 1983; Goldin et al. 1987; McGuffin and Sturt 1986) to warrant futher investigation. Other genetic marker loci (e.g., Gc, Gm, Km, complement C4B, and C3) have also been reported to be associated with schizophrenia in single studies, although they remain unconfirmed (Book et al. 1978; McGuffin and Sturt 1986; Rudduck et al. 1985a, 1985b). Evidence for linkage of a spectrum of depressive disorder with C3 (Tanna et al. 1976a) and pure depressive disorder with Gc (Tanna et al. 1976b) also exist. The other isolated association and linkage studies in affective disorder are reviewed in Hill et al. (1988). However, these genetic marker studies, all reported before the application of restriction fragment length polymorphism (RFLP) marker studies to human disease, do not appear to be useful leads.

CYTOGENETIC STUDIES (CHROMOSOMAL IDENTIFICATION)

Previous chromosomal studies of psychiatric hospitalized patients, although based on large populations, remain inconclusive. Most are extensive surveys of all hospitalized patients and have not utilized systematically defined diagnostic criteria. In addition, in the majority of studies, complete karyotypes of patients were not performed; only the X chromosome number was assessed by examining buccal smears.

A summary of these data (reviewed by DeLisi et al. 1988a) suggests that there is a modest excess of XXY males and XXX females among psychiatric hospital patients, although these aberrations in no way account for the vast majority of major psychiatric illnesses. Case reports also exist of schizophrenic-like symptoms in patients with known Klinefelter (XXY) and triple X syndromes (reviewed in Forssman 1970; Money and Hirsch 1963; Polani 1969). Similarly, manic-depression has been described in Klinefelter's cases (Caroff 1978; Lesage and Chouinard 1978), and rare anomalies with several extra X and Y chromosomes (Jancar 1968; Singh and Rajkoma 1986). Turner's syndrome (XO) also has been reported in association with affective disorder, but not schizophrenia (Fishbain and Vilasuso 1981; Larocca 1985). No study to date, however, has reported the prevalence statistics for psychosis in any of these patient groups with the X anomalies. There is also no existing hypothesis that has been put forth to explain why the presence of an extra dose of genes on the X chromosome could lead to psychosis, particularly if inactivation of the extra X chromosomes takes place at the cellular level. While the location of a psychosis gene could be deduced from these data to be within the pseudoautosomal region of the X chromosome, where inactivation does not take place (Crow 1987, 1988), there are still no clues to the nature of the gene.

Another genetic condition linked to an X chromosome abnormality that has gained recent attention in psychiatry is the fragile site mapped to the Xq27 region (end of the long arm). The presence of the fragile site is now known to be associated with approximately 30% to 50% of all X-linked mental retardation in males (Turner et al. 1978) and 4% to 5% of all mental retardation in males (Rogers and Simensen 1987; Webb et al. 1987). This form of mental retardation, named the Martin-Bell syndrome after its first describers (Martin and Bell 1943), is clinically characterized by mild dysmorphic facial features (long narrow facies, large ears) and other physical anomalies, including macroorchidism and joint hyperextensibility. Fragile X males and females have also been reported to show autistic and psychotic symptoms. An excess of fragile X has been reported among children diagnosed with autism as well (Brown et al. 1986). Systematic family diagnostic studies suggest that the female carriers of the fragile X site may have increased prevalence of schizoaffective disorder and schizophrenia spectrum personality disorders (Reiss et al. 1986, 1988).

Other miscellaneous chromosomal anomalies have been described in several isolated unconfirmed reports. One study described an unusually high percentage of aberrations (approximately 30%) among patients with paranoid psychoses (Axelsson and Wahlstrom 1984). These include long Y chromosomes, duplications in the heterochromatin regions of several chromosomes, inversion of a region on chromosome 9, and fragile sites on chromosomes 17 and 9. Rudduck and Franzen (1983) found an association between a fragile site on the long arm of chromosome 3 and schizophrenia. Another fragile site on chromosome 19 was seen in schizophrenic members within one family (Chodirker et al. 1987). Both trisomy 8 (Sperber 1975) and trisomy of a portion of the long arm of chromosome 5 (Bassett et al. 1988), as well as a balanced translocation of the distal long arm of 2 (Genest et al. 1976), have also been associated with schizophrenia. Thus no consistent pattern of chromosomal abnormalities has emerged. Nevertheless, some investigators assume that these abnormalities may each be markers of regions of the genome to investigate further in the search for the putative psychosis gene. Others argue that this strategy, while successful in a couple of disease investigations, is unlikely to be fruitful; many miscellaneous illnesses have been associated with chromosomal anomalies that have not led to the correct chromosomal region eventually linked to the disease. Perhaps, however, these reports will at least initiate searches for a gene that, while only defective in rare cases of schizophrenia, is part of a common pathway underlying the pathogenesis of the disorder. Other genes influencing this pathway may be also found on other chromosomes.

MOLECULAR GENETIC LINKAGE STUDIES

Using cloned DNA probes for specific loci, the genome can now be scanned for disease markers (reviewed in Baron and Rainer 1988; Gershon et al. 1987; White 1984). This recombinant DNA approach is based on the existence of DNA sequence variations in different individuals that can be detected because they may alter the recognition site of restriction endonucleases enzymes, which catalyze specific breaks in double-stranded DNA. Using multiple probes for loci on different chromosomes, it is possible to identify a specific region that is linked to a disease locus before identifying the defective gene.

DNA is generally prepared from whole blood or lymphocytes from individuals; commonly, the lymphocytes are transformed in culture with Epstein-Barr virus, which ensures continuous growth of the cells. Thus established lines can be stored and grown indefinitely to replenish supplies of DNA for multiple studies. DNA is then isolated from these cells in a series of routine extraction procedures that most recently has even been automated and preparable by laboratory "robots." The DNA is cut into fragments by restriction enzymes (which recognize specific base-pair sequences for their breaking points) and separated by gel electrophoresis. The fragments are then fixed by transfer to a nylon or nitrocellulose blot (Southern transfer blot) and probed with labeled cloned DNA, which marks a specific locus. Autoradiographs of these fragments can then be visualized and scored for each individual (specific procedures are outlined in Maniatis et al. 1982). Variations in the DNA are detected as a change in fragment profile. These diverse patterns are heritable and referred to as restriction fragment length polymorphisms (RFLPs).

Many inherited disorders have already been linked to specific genes using this methodology. Of particular interest to neuropsychiatry is the linkage of a locus on the distal short arm of chromosome 4 to Huntington's disease (Gusella et al. 1983), and the linkage of Alzheimer's disease to an amyloid linked marker on chromosome 21 (Tanzi et al. 1987). Feder et al. (1985) were the first to publish any RFLP examinations of psychiatric patients with their attempt to test the hypothesis that endogenous opiate production was abnormal in psychotic disorders. They failed to find any associations of RFLPs of the opiate precursor, the propiomelanocortin gene, with schizophrenia or bipolar illness. Over the past few years other preliminary studies using some cell lines from patients with schizophrenia (described in DeLisi et al. 1987b) were similarly performed. These studies made use of identified polymorphisms for several other neuropeptides and related substances (Detera-Wadleigh et al. 1986, 1987, unpublished data). Groups of unrelated schizophrenic and bipolar patients were compared with screened controls to look for rare polymorphisms that were more frequent among patient groups. No such associations were found when using cloned probes for neuropeptide Y, somatostatin, substance P, gastrin-releasing peptide, vasoactive intestinal peptide (VIP), insulin, HRAS1, tyrosine hydroxylase, and phenylalanine hydroxylase. Only a polymorphism in the adenosine deaminase gene was significantly more frequent in schizophrenic patients compared with controls ($\chi^2 = 4.09, p < .05$), but it has yet to be examined in a larger population, probably because little clinical relevance seems apparent in this chance finding.

A linkage of manic-depressive illness in a large Amish family to a region of chromosome 11 near the HRAS1, insulin, and tyrosine hydroxylase genes (Egeland et al. 1987), as well as in other pedigrees to the long arm of the X chromosome (Mendlewicz et al. 1987), gained wide interest in 1986 as the first report of a clear linkage to a chromosomal region in a psychiatric disorder. However, subsequent attempts to generalize this finding to other families with bipolar disorder, schizoaffective disorder, or schizophrenid have not so far been successful (Byerley et al. 1988; Detera-Wadleigh et al. unpublished data).

X-chromosome linkage has often been thought to be more relevant to affective disorder than schizophrenia, based on segregation analyses of large pedigrees and the rarity of father-to-son transmission, suggesting partial X linkage or X linkage in subgroups of families (Reich et al. 1969; Winokur and Tanna 1969). Linkage of bipolar disorder to deutan color blindness (mapped to the distal region of the long arm of the X chromosome) has been controversial. One group (Baron et al. 1987) maintained that this linkage does exist, whereas others (Gershon et al. 1979; Kidd et al. 1984; Leckman et al. 1979) failed to find this linkage in any of their families studied. Nevertheless, confirmation of Baron et al.'s studies comes from a recent Belgian report of linkage to the factor 8 blood group gene (using the RFLP methodology) in families with bipolar disorder (Mendlewicz et al. 1987). While we have thus far failed to find any evidence of this linkage in families with schizophrenia (DeLisi et al. 1988b), the clinical data from studies of families with fragile X (a region tightly linked to the above-studied markers) provide further evidence that this area of the X chromosome is worth continued investigation.

There has recently been a report by Sherington et al. (1988) of a linkage of schizophrenia in seven families from Iceland and the United Kingdom to a region on the proximal long arm of the 5th chromosome. It is particularly noteworthy that linkage was strongest when a broad definition of illness that included all family members with affective disorder was considered in the analysis. In the same issue of *Nature*, however, appeared a second independent study (Kennedy et al. 1988) failing to find a similar linkage in a large pedigree from a genetic isolate in northern Sweden. Linkage studies have also recently been performed in both extended schizophrenia and primarily-bipolar families from the United States (Detera-Wadleigh et al. 1989, and unpublished observations; Kaufmann et al., in press) using a probe for the glucocorticoid receptor mapped to the distal portion of the long arm of chromosome 5 and several polymorphic markers in the region more proximal reported to be associated with the translocation previously described (Bassett et al. 1988). These studies have thus far not resulted in a positive linkage of schizophrenia or affective disorder to this region. A suggestion of possible linkage to an area of chromosome 2 in four families with schizophrenia was described using a highly variable cDNA probe mapped to an area with unknown function or clinical relevance (Cloninger 1988). This is particularly interesting in view of the one report of an association of schizophrenia with a translocation from the same general area of chromosome 2 (Genest et al. 1976).

Thus, with the exception of the Huntington's disease finding (Gusella et al. 1983), none of these several recent reports on neuropsychiatric disorders have been confirmed in a wide sample of families with the same illness. They remain isolated suggestions that have yet to be generalized to other samples of families and thus considered as definitive locations for the gene. There are still several other candidate regions of the genome that are worth pursuit in both disorders. These include those regions where genes related to some of the neurochemical pathways involved with the previously mentioned findings are located.

Summary of Potential Candidate Genes for Future RFLP Studies

Since it is possible that major psychiatric disorders may be linked to genes for a variety of substances related to brain metabolism, growth, and development, probes for these substances (when available) or probes closely linked to these substances (when available from other research laboratories) can be used in hybridization studies (Table 6).

Enzymes. Both catecholamine and indolamine neurotransmitters and related substances have been found to be abnormally concentrated in blood, CSF, and brain in psychiatric disorders. These findings (see DeLisi 1987) could be explained by defects in enzymes catalyzing their synthesis or metabolism. The issues raised by past studies showing reduced peripheral measures of both MAO and

Table 6. Proposed Candidate Genes and Their Locations, as Established by the Human Gene Mapping Collaborative Workshops

Candidate factors	Chromosome location	Known RFLPs
Enzymes		
Monoamine oxidase	X	No
Catecholamine-O-methyl transferase	22	No
Dopamine B-hydroxylase	9	No
Tyrosine hydroxylase	11p15.5	Yes
Phenylalanine hydroxylase	12p22-q24.2	Yes
Neuropeptides		
Cholecystokinin	3	No
Vasoactive intestinal peptide	6	No
NPY	7pter-q22	Yes
Neurotensin	—	Yes
Somatostatin	3q28	Yes
Receptors		
Dopamine	—	
Serotonin	—	
Alpha-adrenergic	—	
Beta-2-adrenergic	5q31-q32	Yes
Nerve growth factor receptor	17q22	Yes
Miscellaneous		
Huntington's disease linked probe	4	Yes
Probes on proximal portion of long arm (q11.2-q13)	5	Yes
Nerve growth factor (beta)	1p22.1	Yes
Growth factors/oncogenes	several	
Fragile site	Xq27	Yes
Pseudoautosomal region	Xp telomeric	Yes

Note. Information obtained from Howard Hughes Medical Institute Human Gene Mapping Library, Yale University, New Haven, CT. NPY = neuropeptide Y; RFLP = restriction fragment length polymorphisms.

dopamine beta-hydroxylase in schizophrenic patients have not been resolved. Catecholamine-O-methyl transferase is another major enzyme involved in the metabolism of dopamine and norepinephrine, both neurotransmitters hypothesized to be in excess in some forms of schizophrenia. Tyrosine hydroxylase is the enzyme involved in the rate-limiting step in dopamine synthesis. In addition, phenylalanine hydroxylase, the enzyme deficient in patients with phenylketonuria (PKU), has been hypothesized to play a role in schizophrenia and affective disorder based on several studies of serum phenylalanine and phenylethylamine concentrations in patients with these disorders (DeLisi and Wyatt 1987).

Both A and B forms of MAO have been mapped in humans to the proximal short arm of the X chromosome and cloned (Bach et al. 1988; Ozelius et al. 1988). Tyrosine hydroxylase has been mapped to the distal short arm of chromosome 11; phenylalanine hydroxylase has been similarly mapped to the short arm of the 12th chromosome, cloned, and used in some of the first reported human RFLP studies (Woo et al. 1983). PKU, which has long been known to be due to a deficiency in phenylalanine hydroxylase activity, is now detectable prenatally using polymorphisms identified with probes for this gene (Woo et al. 1986).

Neuropeptides.   Several of the neuropeptides have been found to coexist with catecholamines intraneuronally and have modulating effects on their activity (reviewed in Cooper et al. 1982). Some—such as cholecystokinin (CCK) and somatostatin (SOM)—have also been found to be in abnormal concentrations in regions of postmortem brain of schizophrenic patients (Roberts et al. 1983).

Receptors.   Numerous studies (pharmacological, physiological, clinical, postmortem, and, most recently, in vivo PET) have implicated abnormalities of dopamine receptors in schizophrenia (reviewed in Crow and Deakin 1985). Thus when the dopamine receptor is cloned and human cDNA probes available, linkage to this gene would be worth examination. Other receptors, such as the noradrenergic and the serotinergic receptor types, may also be worth studying.

Growth factors.   It has been suggested that psychosis may be associated with abnormal regulation or production of a cellular growth factor, which determines the asymmetries in human brain, since disturbances of normal brain laterality have been noted in schizophrenia (Crow 1984). For this reason, growth factors could also be considered as potential candidate genes.

Miscellaneous.   Patients with Huntington's disease may, as part of their clinical spectrum of symptoms, exhibit psychotic behavior sometimes misdiagnosed as schizophrenia, as well as major affective disorder. Although these disorders and Huntington's disease obviously do not result from the same mutation, it is still possible that they might be allelic or that their loci may be linked on the same chromosome. As mentioned above, Bassett et al. (1988) described the presence of a translocation of the q11-13 portion of the proximal long arm of chromosome 5 to chromosome 1 in two schizophrenic members of one pedigree. Other chromosomal aberrations have also been reported. While it is unlikely that schizophrenia is due to such anomalies in a substantial portion of cases, these findings may suggest that loci in those regions could be associated with some cases of schizophrenia.

Another possibility that has been proposed to account for apparently variable X linkage for psychoses and the frequent associations of X chromosome anomalies to schizophrenia is that the locus may be situated within the pseudoautosomal region of the sex chromosomes. This is a region at the distal end of the short arms of the X and Y chromosomes with a gradient of completely autosomal-like recombinational events between both chromosomes at the distal end to almost no crossing over at the proximal end, thus enabling defects on the X chromosome to be transmitted by the Y chromosome in a "pseudoautosomal" fashion or as partially X linked (Page et al. 1987; Rouyer et al. 1986a, 1986b). This is also the only region of the X chromosome that does not undergo the usual inactivation process that takes place in individuals with more than one X chromosome. Thus, in the case of Klinefelter (XXY) males and triple X (XXX) females, the pseudoautosomal region of the X chromosome specifically is functionally in excess and may explain the association of psychosis with these syndromes. Clinical information on the pattern of inheritance in pairs of schizophrenic siblings has been shown to be consistent with inheritance in the pseudoautosomal region (Crow et al. in press). While several previous studies of sibling pairs showed significantly greater same sex than opposite sex concordance for schizophrenia (DeLisi et al. 1987b; Penrose 1945; Schulz 1932; Tsuang 1967; Zehnder 1941), the above analysis found that this same sex concordance rate was specifically relevant when inheritance of illness was from the paternal, but not the maternal, side of the family. This particular pattern could be specific to inheritance of a gene within the pseudoautosomal region, since when carried on the X chromosome from the father it must be transmitted only to daughters unless recombination occurs in meiosis, and similarly when on the Y it will most likely be transmitted only to sons. In the case of maternal transmission, however, opposite sex siblings with illness are just as likely as same sex siblings, since mothers can transmit the same X equally to sons and daughters. Thus polymorphic probes for this region (already available) will enable the testing of this hypothesis. Same sex concordance has also been reported in studies of siblings with affective disorder (reviewed in Crow 1988). Thus, taken together with the other consistent clinical data, this hypothesis could also be extended to include affective disorders.

CONCLUSION

A genetic vulnerability for major psychiatric illness, including schizophrenia and affective disorders, seems likely, although the details of the underlying mechanisms for such remain unknown. Several putative biological markers of illness have been found frequently in both patients with schizophrenia and patients with affective disorder. These are contrasted in both illnesses above and include abnormalities in catecholamine and indolamine metabolism, possibly receptor function and structure, and other miscellaneous neurochemical and brain morphological measurements common to both disorders, as well as particular X chromosomal abnormalities. Markers that appear specific to one or the other illness may not have been studied extensively in both to conclude that they differentiate the two syndromes. With the availability of new technology to examine the human genome, the search for putative genes has accelerated. The finding of a linked genetic sequence can be the first step in the process to determine the pathological mechanism (such as abnormalities in metabolism of some of the substances mentioned above) for which the defective gene is responsible. Using these techniques, knowing the actual inherited defect no longer is necessary at the onset. In fact, a few suggestions of chromosomal regions for linkage have already emerged. These include regions of the 5th, 11th, and X chromosomes, among others. Some of the linkage data already accumulating suggest that the diagnostic boundaries of homogeneous genetically determined psychiatric illness may have to undergo considerable change, since they appear to include heterogeneous clinical syndromes by present diagnostic classification systems. It is possible that both spectra of schizophrenic and affective syndromes may be inherited through the same genetic locus or sets of related loci, either by variations in the specific mutation(s) responsible for disease in one locus, or by mutations in different but tightly linked or functionally related genes.

REFERENCES

Aberg-Wistedt A, Wistedt B, Bertilsson L: High CSF levels of HVA and 5-HIAA in delusional compared to nondelusional depression. Arch Gen Psychiatry 42:925–926, 1985

Agren H: Symptom patterns in unipolar and bipolar depression correlating with monoamine metabolites in the cerebrospinal fluid: I, general patterns. Psychiatry Res 3:211–224, 1980

American Psychiatric Association: Diagnostic and Statistical Manual of Mental Disorders, Third Edition. Washington, DC, American Psychiatric Association, 1980

Angst J, Felder W, Lohmeyer B: Schizoaffective disorders: results of a genetic investigation. J Affective Disord 1:139–153, 1979

Angst J, Frey R, Lohmeyer B, et al: Bipolar manic-depressive psychoses: results of a genetic investigation. Hum Genet 55:237–254, 1980

Arana GW, Baldessarini RJ: Clinical use of the dexamethasone suppression test in psychiatry, in Psychopharmacology: The Third Generation of Progress. Edited by Meltzer HY. New York, Raven Press, 1987, pp 609–616

Asberg M, Bertilsson L, Bartensson B, et al: CSF monoamine metabolites in melancholia. Acta Psychiatr Scand 69:201–219, 1984

Axelsson R, Wahlstrom J: Chromosome aberrations in patients with paranoid psychosis. Hereditas 100:19–31, 1984

Azumi K: A polygraphic study of sleep in schizophrenics. Seishin Shinkeigaku Zasshi 68:69–75, 1966

Bach AWJ, Lan NC, Johnson DL, et al: cDNA cloning of human liver monoamine oxidase A and B: molecular basis of differences in enzymatic properties. Proc Natl Acad Sci USA 85:4934–4938, 1988

Banki CM, Vojnik M, Molnar G: Cerebrospinal fluid amine metabolites, tryptophan and clinical parameters in depression. J Affect Disord 3:81–89, 1981a

Banki CM, Molnar G, Fekete I: Correlation of individual symptoms and other clinical variables with cerebral spinal fluid amine metabolites and tryptophan in depression. Archiv Für Psychiatrie und Nervenkrankheitan 229:345–353, 1981b

Baron M, Rainer JD: Molecular genetics and human disease: implications for modern psychiatric research and practice. Br J Psychiatry 152:741–753, 1988

Baron M, Gruen R, Asnis L, et al: Schizoaffective disorders, schizophrenia, and affective disorders: morbidity risk and genetic transmission. Acta Psychiatr Scand 65:253–262, 1982

Baron M, Gruen R, Rainer JD, et al: A family study of schizophrenia and normal control probands: implications for the spectrum concept of schizophrenia. Am J Psychiatry 142:447–454, 1985

Baron M, Risch N, Hamberger R, et al: Genetic linkage between X chromosome markers and bipolar affective illness. Nature 326:289–292, 1987

Bassett AS, McGillivray BC, Jones BD, et al: Partial trisomy chromosome 5 cosegregating with schizophrenia. Lancet 1:799–801, 1988

Berger PA, Faull KF, Kilkowski J, et al: CSF monoamine metabolites in depression and schizophrenia. Am J Psychiatry 137:174–180, 1980

Bertelsen A: A Danish twin study of manic-depressive disorder, in Origin, Prevention and Treatment of Affective Disorders. Edited by Shou M, Stromgren E. London, Academic Press, 1979, pp 227–239

Bertelsen A, Harvald B, Hauge M: A Danish twin study of manic-depressive disorders. Br J Psychiatry 130:330–351, 1977

Blehar MC, Weissman MM, Gershon ES, et al: Family and genetic studies of affective disorders. Arch Gen Psychiatry 45:289–292, 1988

Bondy B, Ackenheil M: ^{3}H-Spiperone binding sites in lymphocytes as possible vulnerability marker in schizophrenia. J Psychiatr Res 21:521–529, 1987

Book JA, Wetterberg L, Modrzewska K: Schizophrenia in a north Swedish geographical isolate, 1900–1917: epidemiology, genetics, and biochemistry. Clin Genet 14:373–394, 1978

Brown WT, Jenkins EC, Cohen IL, et al: Fragile X and autism: a mutlicenter survey. Am J Med Genet 23:341–352, 1986

Bucher KD, Elston RC: The transmission of manic-depressive illness: I, theory, description of the model and summary of results. J Psychiatr Res 16:53–63, 1981

Bucher KD, Elston RC, Green R, et al: The transmission of manic-depressive illness: II, segregation analysis of three sets of family data. J Psychiatr Res 16:65–78, 1981

Byerley WF, LaLouel JM, Holik JJ, et al: Utah molecular genetic study of schizophrenia. Presented at annual meeting of the American Psychiatric Association, New Research, Montreal, May 1988

Caroff S: Klinefelter's syndrome and bipolar affective illness: a case report. Am J Psychiatry 135:748–749, 1978

Carter CL, Chung CS: Segregation analysis of schizophrenia under a mixed genetic model. Hum Hered 30:350–356, 1980

Chodirker BN, Chudley AE, Ray M, et al: Fragile 19p13 in a family with mental illness. Clin Genet 31:1–6, 1987

Clayton P: Family study of patients with bipolar and unipolar affective disorders. Paper presented at the National Institute of Mental Health Workshop on Family and Genetic Studies of Affective Disorders, Bethesda, MD, 1986

Cloninger R: Linkage studies in schizophrenia and affective disorders. Presented at the 27th annual meeting of the American College of Neuropsychopharmacology, San Juan, December 1988

Cooper JR, Bloom FE, Roth RH: Neuroactive peptides, in The Biochemical Basis of Neuropharmacology, Fourth Edition. New York, Oxford University Press, 1982, pp 295–320

Crow TJ: A reevaluation of the viral hypothesis: is psychosis the result of retroviral integration at a site close to the cerebral dominance gene. Br J Psychiatry 145:243–253, 1984

Crow TJ: The continuum of psychosis and its implication for the structure of the gene. Br J Psychiatry 149:419–428, 1986

Crow TJ: Pseudoautosomal locus for psychoses? Lancet 2:1532, 1987

Crow TJ: Sex chromosomes and psychosis: the case for a pseudoautosomal locus. Br J Psychiatry 153:675–683, 1988

Crow TJ, Deakin JFW: Neurotransmitters, behavior, and mental disorder, in Handbook of Psychiatry, Vol 5. Edited by Shephard M. Cambridge, Cambridge University Press, 1985, pp 137–182

Crow TJ, Done DJ: Age of onset of schizophrenia in siblings: a test of the contagion hypothesis. Psychiatry Res 18:107–117, 1986

Crow TJ, Johnstone EC: Schizophrenia: nature of the disease process and its biological correlates, in Handbook of Physiology. The Nervous System V. Edited by Plum, EF. Bethesda, MD, American Physiological Society, 1987, pp 843–869

Crow TJ, DeLisi LE, Johnstone EC: Clues to the nature and location of the psychosis gene: is schizophrenia due to an anomaly of the cerebral dominance gene located in the pseudoautosomal region of the sex chromosomes? in Genetics of Neuropsychiatric Diseases. Wenner-Gren Center International Symposium No. 51. Edited by Wetterberg L. New York, Stockton Press (in press)

Crowe RR, Naboodiri KK, Ashby HB, et al: Segregation and linkage analysis of a large kindred of unipolar depression. Neuropsychobiology 7:20–25, 1981

DeLisi LE, Crow TJ, Davies K, et al: The X chromosome and psychiatric disorders: cytogenetic and molecular studies. Presented at the 27th annual meeting of the American College of Psychopharmacology, San Juan, Puerto Rico, December 1988b

DeLisi LE, Alexandropoulos A, Colter N, et al: Reduced temporal lobe area: an MRI study of siblings with schizophrenia. Schizophrenia Res 1:169–170, 1988c

DeLisi LE, Goldin LR, Gershon ES: Studies of biological factors associated with the inheritance of schizophrenia: a selective review. J Psychiatr Res 21:507–513, 1987a

DeLisi LE, Goldin LR, Hamovit JR, et al: A family study of the association of increased ventricular size with schizophrenia. Arch Gen Psychiatry 43:148–153, 1986

DeLisi LE, Goldin LR, Maxwell ME, et al: Clinical features of illness in siblings with schizophrenia or schizoaffective disorder. Arch Gen Psychiatry 44:891–896, 1987b

DeLisi LE, Karoum F, Targum S, et al: The determination of urinary 3-methoxy-4-hydroxyphenylglycol excretion in acute schizophreniform and depressed patients. Biol Psychiatry 18:1189–1196, 1983

DeLisi LE, Neckers LM, Weinberger D, et al: Increased whole blood serotonin concentrations in chronic schizophrenic patients. Arch Gen Psychiatry 38:647–650, 1981a

DeLisi LE, Reiss AL, White BJ, et al: Cytogenetic studies of males with schizophrenia: screening for the fragile X chromosome and other chromosomal abnormalities. Schizophrenia Research 1:277–281, 1988a

DeLisi LE, Wise CD, Bridge TP, et al: Monoamine oxidase and schizophrenia, in Biological Markers in Psychiatry and Neurology. Edited by Usdin E, Hamin I. Oxford, Pergamon Press, 1982, pp 79–96

DeLisi LE, Wise CD, Bridge TP, et al: A probable neuroleptic effect on platelet monoamine oxidase activity. Psychiatry Res 4:95–107, 1981b

DeLisi LE, Wise CD, Phelps BH, et al: Dopamine B-hydroxylase, monoamine oxidase and schizophrenia. Biol Psychiatry 15:899–905, 1980

DeLisi LE, Wyatt RJ: Neurochemical aspects of schizophrenia, in Handbook of Neurochemistry, Vol 10. Edited by Lajtha JR. New York, Plenum, 1985, pp 553–587

DeLisi LE, Wyatt RJ: Endogenous hallucinogens and other behavior modifying factors in schizophrenia, in Neurochemistry and Neuropharmacology of Schizophrenia. Edited by Henn FA, DeLisi LE. Amsterdam, Elsevier, 1987, pp 377–390

Dement W: Dream recall and eye movements during sleep in schizophrenics and normals. J Nerv Ment Dis 122:263–369, 1955

Detera-Wadleigh S, DeLisi LE, Berrettini WH, et al: DNA polymorphisms in schizophrenia and affective disorders, in Proceedings of the IVth World Congress of Biological Psychiatry. Edited by Shagass C, Josiassen RC, Bridger WH, et al. New York, Elsevier, 1986, pp 67–69

Detera-Wadleigh SD, de Miguel C, Berrettini WH, et al: Neuropeptide gene polymorphisms in affective disorder and schizophrenia. J Psychiatr Res 21:581–587, 1987

Detera-Wadleigh SD, Goldin LR, Sherrington R, et al: Exclusion of linkage to 5q11-13 in families with schizophrenia and other psychiatric disorders. Nature 340:391–393, 1989

Dorus E, Pandey GN, Shaughnessey R, Lithium transport across the RBC membrane. Arch Gen Psychiatry 37:80–81, 1980

Egeland JR, Gerrhard DS, Pauls DL, et al: Bipolar affective disorders linked to DNA markers on chromosome 11. Nature 325:783–787, 1987

Erlenmeyer-Kimling L: Biological markers for the liability to schizophrenia, in Biological Perspectives in Schizophrenia: Dahlem Workshop reports LS 40. Edited by Helmchen H, Henn FA. Cambridge, Wiley & Sons, 1987, pp 33–56

Farde L, Wiesel F-A, Hall H, et al: No D_2 receptor increase in PET study of schizophrenia. Arch Gen Psychiatry 44:671–672, 1987

Feder J, Gurling HMD, Darby J, et al: DNA restriction fragment analysis of the proopiomelanocortin gene in schizophrenia and bipolar disorders. Am J Hum Genet 37:286–294, 1985

Feinberg I, Koresko R, Gottleib F, et al: Sleep electroencephalographic and eye movement patterns in schizophrenic patients. Compr Psychiatry 5:44–53, 1964

Fishbain DA, Vilasuso A: Manic-depressive illness associated with Turner's syndrome mosaicism. J Nerv Ment Dis 169:459–461, 1981

Flemenbaum A, Larson JW: ABO-Rh blood groups and psychiatric diagnosis: a critical review. Diseases of the Nervous System 37:581–583, 1976

Forssman H: The mental implications of sex chromosome aberrations. Br J Psychiatry 117:353–363, 1970

Genest P, Dumas L, Genest FB: Translocation chromosomique t(2;18) (q21;q23) chez un individual schizophrene et sa fille. L'Union Medicale du Canada 105:1617–1681, 1976

Gershon ES, Goldin LR: The outlook for linkage research in psychiatric disorders. J Psychiatr Res 21:541–550, 1987

Gershon ES, Baron M, Leckman JF: Genetic models of the transmission of affective disorders. J Psychiatr Res 12:301–317, 1975

Gershon ES, Bunney WE Jr, Leckman JF, et al: The inheritance of affective disorders: a review of data and hypotheses. Behav Genet 6:227–261, 1976

Gershon ES, Targum SD, Kessler LR, et al: Genetic studies and biologic strategies in the affective disorders, in Progress in Medical Genetics, Vol 2. Edited by Steinberg AG, Bearn AG, Motulsky AG, et al. Philadelphia, WB Saunders Co, 1977, pp 101–164

Gershon ES, Targum SD, Matthyssee S, et al: Color blindness not closely linked to bipolar illness: report of a new pedigree series. Arch Gen Psychiatry 36:1423–1434, 1979

Gershon ES, Hamovit J, Guroff JJ, et al: A family study of schizoaffective, bipolar I, bipolar II, unipolar, and normal control probands. Arch Gen Psychiatry 39:1157–1167, 1982

Gershon ES, Merrill CR, Goldin LR, et al: The role of molecular genetics in psychiatry. Biol Psychiatry 22:1388–1405, 1987

Gershon ES, DeLisi LE, Maxwell ME, et al: A family study of schizophrenia and schizoaffective disorder. Arch Gen Psychiatry 45:328–337, 1988

Goldin LR, Gershon ES: Association and linkage studies of genetic marker loci in major psychiatric disorders. Psychiatr Dev 4:387–418, 1983

Goldin LR, Kidd KK, Matthysse S, et al: The power of pedigree segregation analysis for traits with incomplete penetrance, in Genetic Strategies in Psychobiology and Psychiatry. Edited by Gershon ES, Matthysse S, Ciaranello RD, et al. Pacific Grove, Calif, Boxwood Press, 1981, pp 305–317

Goldin LR, Clerget-Darpoux F, Gershon ES: Relationship of HLA to major affective disorder not supported. Psychiatry Res 7:29–45, 1982

Goldin LR, Gershon ES, Targum SD, et al: Segregation and linkage analyses in families of patients with bipolar, unipolar, and schizoaffective mood disorders. Am J Hum Genet 35:274–287, 1983

Goldin LR, Cox NJ, Pauls DL, et al: The detection of major loci by segregation and linkage analysis: a stimulation study. Genetic Epidemiology 1:285–296, 1984

Goldin LR, DeLisi LE, Gershon ES: The relation of HLA to schizophrenia in 10 nuclear families. Psychiatry Res 20:69–77, 1987

Gottesman II, Shields J: Schizophrenia: The Epigenetic Puzzle. New York, Cambridge University Press, 1982

Gottfries C-G, Oreland L, Wiberg A, et al: Lowered monoamine oxidase activity in brains from alcoholic suicides. J Neurochem 25:667–673, 1975

Grote SS, Moses SG, Robins E, et al: A study of selected catecholamine metabolizing enzymes: A comparison of depressive suicides and alcoholic suicides with controls. J Neurochem 23:791–802, 1974

Gulevich G, Dement W, Zarcone V: All-night sleep recordings of chronic schizophrenics in remission. Compr Psychiatry 8:148–149, 1967

Gusella JF, Wexler NS, Conneally PM, et al: A polymorphic DNA marker genetically linked to Huntington's disease. Nature 306:234–238, 1983

Guze SB, Cloninger CR, Martin RL, et al: A follow-up and family study of schizophrenia. Arch Gen Psychiatry 40:1273–1276, 1983

Hauser P: Presented at the annual meeting of The American Psychiatric Association, New Research. Montreal, Canada, May 1988

Hill EM, Wilson AF, Elston RC, et al: Evidence for possible linkage between genetic markers and affective disorders. Biol Psychiatry 24:903–917, 1988

Holzman PS: Eye movement dysfunction and psychosis. Int Rev Neurobiol 27:179–205, 1985

Holzman PS, Proctor LR, Levy DL, et al: Eye-tracking dysfunctions in schizophrenic patients and their relatives. Arch Gen Psychiatry 31:143–151, 1974

Holzman PS, Kringlen E, Levy DL, et al: Deviant eye-tracking in twins discordant for psychosis: a replication. Arch Gen Psychiatry 32:627–631, 1980

Jancar J: XXYY with manic-depression. Lancet 2:970, 1968

Johnstone EC, Owens DGC, Crow TJ, et al: Temporal lobe structure as determined by nuclear magnetic resonance in schizophrenia and bipolar affective disorder. J Neurol Neurosurg Psychiatry 52:736–741, 1989

Kaufmann CA, Gillin JC, Hill B, et al: Muscarinic binding in suicides. Psychiatry Res 12:47–56, 1984

Kendler KS: Overview: a current perspective on twin studies of schizophrenia. Am J Psychiatry 140:1413–1425, 1983

Kendler KS, Masterson CC, Davis KL: Psychiatric illness in first-degree relatives of patients with paranoid psychoses, schizophrenia, and medical illness. Br J Psychiatry 147:524–530, 1985

Kennedy JL, Gluffrat LA, Moises HW, et al: Evidence against linkage of schizophrenia to markers on chromosome 5 in a Northern Swedish pedigree. Nature 336:167–170, 1988

Kety SS: Disorders of the human brain: they can result from inherited metabolic defect, vascular disease, infection, tumor, and trauma. Sci Am 241:202–218, 1979

Kety SS, Rosenthal D, Wender PH, et al: Mental illness in the biologic and adoptive families of adopted individuals who become schizophrenic: a preliminary report based on psychiatric interviews, in Genetic Research in Psychiatry. Edited by Fieve RR, Rosenthal D, Brill H. Baltimore, Johns Hopkins University Press, 1975, pp 147–165

Kidd KK, Egeland JL, Molthan L, et al: Amish study IV: genetic linkage study of pedigrees of bipolar probands. Am J Psychiatry 141:1042–1048, 1984

Klerman GL, Lavori P, Rice J, et al. Birth-cohort trends in rates of major depressive disorder among relatives of patients with affective disorder. Arch Gen Psychiatry 42:689–693, 1985

Ko GN, Korpi ER, Freed WJ, et al: Effect of valproic acid on behavior and plasma amino-acid concentrations in chronic schizophrenic patients. Biol Psychiatry 20:209–215, 1985

Koslow SH, Maas JW, Bowden CL, et al: CSF and urinary biogenic amines and metabolites: depression and mania: a controlled univariate analysis. Arch Gen Psychiatry 40:999–1010, 1983

Kraepelin E: Lehrbuich der Psychiatrie. Translated by Diefendorf AR. New York, Macmillan, 1907

Kraepelin E: Manic-depressive insanity and paranoia. Salem, NH, Ayer Co. 1921

Larocca FE: Concurrence of Turner's syndrome, anorexia nervosa, and mood disorders: case report. J Clin Psychiatry 46:296–297, 1985

Leckman JF, Gershon ES, McGinniss MH, et al: New data do not suggest linkage between the Xg blood group and bipolar illness. Arch Gen Psychiatry 36:1435–1441, 1979

Lesage J, Chouinard G: Manic-depressive illness associated with Klinefelter's syndrome and essential tremors (letter). Am J Psychiatry 135:757–758, 1978

Lipton RB, Levy DL, Holzman PS, et al: Eye movement dysfunctions in psychiatric patients: a review. Schizophr Bull 9:13–22, 1983

Losonczy MF, Davidson M, Davis KL: The dopamine hypothesis of schizophrenia, in Psychopharmacology: The Third Generation of Progress. Edited by Meltzer HY. New York, Raven Press, 1987, pp 715–726.

Macciardi F, Proverza M, Bellodi L, et al: Genetic notes of schizophrenic disorders, in Etiopathogenetic Hypotheses of Schizophrenia. Edited by Cazullo CL, Invernizzi G, Sacchetti E, et al. Lancaster, PA, MTP Press, 1987, pp 21–32.

Maniatis T, Fritsch EF, Sambrook J: Molecular Cloning: A Laboratory Manual. New York, Cold Spring Harbor Laboratory, 1982

Mann JJ, Stanley M: Post-mortem monoamine-oxidase enzyme kinetics in the frontal cortex of suicide victims and controls. Acta Psychiatr Scand 69:135–139, 1984

Martin JB, Bell J: A pedigree of mental defect showing sex linkage. Journal of Neurology and Psychiatry 6:154–157, 1943

Matthysse S, Holzman PS, Lange K: The genetic transmission of schizophrenia: application of Mendelian latent structure analysis to eye-tracking dysfunction in schizophrenia and affective disorder. J Psychiatr Res 20:57–67, 1986

McGue M, Gottesman II, Rao DC: The transmission of schizophrenia under a multifactorial threshold model. Am J Hum Genet 35:1161–1178, 1983

McGue M, Gottesman II, Rao DC: Resolving genetic models for the transmission of schizophrenia. Genetic Epidemiology 2: 99–110, 1985

McGuffin P, Sturt E: Genetic markers in schizophrenia. Hum Hered 36:65–88, 1986

McGuffin P, Festenstein H, Murray R: A family study of HLA antigens and other genetic markers in schizophrenia. Psychol Med 13:31–43, 1983

Mendlewicz J, Rainer JD: Adoption study supporting genetic transmission in manic-depressive illness. Nature 268:327–329, 1977

Mendlewicz J, Sevy S, Brocas H, et al: Polymorphic DNA marker on X chromosome and manic depression. Lancet 1:1230–1232, 1987

Meyerson LR, Wennogle LP, Abel MS, et al: Human brain receptor alterations in suicide victims. Pharmacol Biochem Behav 17:159–163, 1982

Money J, Hirsch SR: Chromosome anomalies, mental deficiency and schizophrenia. Archives of General Psychology 8:54–63, 1963

Nadi NS, Nurnberger JL, Gershon ES: Muscarinic cholinergic receptors on skin fibroblasts in familial affective disorder. N Engl J Med 311:225–230, 1984

Nasrallah HA, McCalley-Whitters M, Phohl B: Clinical significance of large cerebral ventricles in manic males. Psychiatry Res 13:151–156, 1984

Nies A, Robinson DS, Lamborn KR, et al: Genetic control of platelet and plasma monoamine oxidase activity. Arch Gen Psychiatry 28:834–838, 1971

Nurnberger JI Jr, Sitaram N, Gershon ES, et al: A twin study of cholinergic REM induction. Biol Psychiatry 18:116–117, 1983

Oreland L, von Knorring L, Schalling D: Connections between monoamine oxidase, temperament and disease, in Proceedings of the IUPHAR 9th International Congress of Pharmacology, London 1984, Vol 2. Edited by Paton W, Mitchell J, Turner P. London, Macmillan, 1984, pp 193–202

Owen F, Bourne RC, Crow TJ, et al: Platelet monoamine oxidase activity in acute schizophrenia: relationship to symptomatology and neuroleptic medication. Br J Psychiatry 139:16–22, 1981

Oxenstierna G, Edman G, Iselius L, et al: Concentrations of monoamine metabolites in the cerebrospinal fluid of twins and unrelated individuals: a genetic study. J Psychiatr Res 20:19–29, 1986

Ozelius L, Hsu Y-PP, Bruns G, et al: Human monoamine oxidase gene (MAOA): chromosome position (Xp21-p11) and DNA polymorphism. Genomics 3:53–58, 1988

Page DC, Bieker K, Brown LG, et al: Linkage, physical mapping, and DNA sequence analysis of pseudoautosomal loci on the human X and Y chromosomes. Genomics 1:243–256, 1987

Pearlson GD, Garbucz DJ, Breakey WR, et al: Lateral ventricular enlargement associated with persistent unemployment and negative symptoms in both schizophrenia and bipolar disorder. Psychiatry Res 12:1–9, 1986

Penrose LS: Survey of cases of familiar mental illness. Digest of Neurology and Psychiatry 13:644, 1945

Pickar D, Sweeney DR, Maas JW, et al: Primary affective disorder, clinical state change, and MHPG secretion: a longitudinal study. Arch Gen Psychiatry 35:1378–1383, 1978

Polani PE: Abnormal sex chromosomes and mental disorder. Nature 223:680–686, 1969

Post RM, Jimerson DC, Ballenger JC: Cerebral spinal fluid neurepinephrine and its metabolites in manic-depressive illness, in Neurobiology of Mood Disorders. Edited by Post RM, Ballenger JC. Baltimore, MD, Williams & Wilkins, 1984, pp 539–553

Potkin SG, Weinberger DR, Linnoila M, et al: Low CSF 5-hydroxyindolaetic acid in schizophrenic patients with enlarged cerebral ventricles. Am J Psychiatry 140:21–25, 1983

Rao DC, Morton NE, Gottesman II, et al: Path analysis of quantitative data on pairs of relatives: application to schizophrenia. Hum Hered 31:325–333, 1981

Rees L, Butler PWP, Gosling C, et al: Adrenergic blockade and the corticosteroid and growth hormone responses to methylamphetamine. Nature 228:565–566, 1970

Reich T, Clayton PJ, Winokur G: Family history studies: the genetics of mania. Am J Psychiatry 125:1358–1369, 1969

Reich T, Rice J, Van Eerdewegh P: The familial association of bipolar and non-bipolar affective disorders. Paper presented at the National Institute of Mental Health Workshop on Family and Genetic Studies of Affective Disorders, Bethesda, Md, 1986

Reiss AL, Feinstein C, Toomey KE, et al: Psychiatric disability associated with the fragile X chromosome. Am J Med Genet 23:393–402, 1986

Reiss AL, Hagerman RJ, Vinogradov S, et al: Psychiatric disability in female carriers of the fragile X chromosome. Arch Gen Psychiatry 45:25–30, 1988

Reveley AM, Reveley MA, Clifford CA, et al: Cerebral ventricular size in twins discordant for schizophrenia. Lancet 1:540–541, 1982

Reveley MA, Reveley AM, Clifford CA, et al: Genetics of platelet MAO activity in discordant schizophrenic and normal twins. Br J Psychiatry 142:89–93, 1983

Reveley AM, Reveley MA, Murray RM: Cerebral ventricular enlargement in non-genetic schizophrenia: a controlled twin study. Br J Psychiatry 144:89–93, 1984

Rice J, McGuffin P, Goldin LR, et al: Platelet monamine oxidase (MAO) activity: evidence for a single major locus. Am J Hum Genet 36:36–43, 1984

Risch N, Baron M: Segregation analysis of schizophrenia and related disorders. Am J Hum Genet 36:1039–1059, 1984

Roberts GW, Ferrier IN, Lee Y, et al: Peptides, the limbic lobe and schizophrenia. Brain Res 288:199–211, 1983

Rogers RC, Simensen RJ: Fragile X syndrome: a common etiology of mental retardation. Am J Ment Defic 91:445–449, 1987

Rosenthal D: Familial concordance by sex with respect to schizophrenia. Psychol Bull 59:401–421, 1962

Rosenthal D, Wender PH, Kety SS, et al: The adopted away offspring of schizophrenics. Am J Psychiatry 128:397–411, 1971

Rotrosen J, Wolkin A: Phospholipid and prostaglandin hypotheses of schizophrenia, in Psychopharmacology: The Third Generation of Progress. Edited by Meltzer HY. New York, Raven Press, 1987, pp 759–764

Rouyer F, Simmler M-C, Johnsson C, et al: A gradient of sex linkage in the pseudoautosomal region of the human sex chromosomes. Nature 319:291–295, 1986a

Rouyer F, Simmler M-C, Vergnaud G, et al: The pseudoautosomal region of the human sex chromosomes. Cold Spring Harbor Symp Quant Biol 51:221–228, 1986b

Roy A, Pickar D, Linnoila M, et al: Cerebrospinal fluid monoamine and monoamine metabolite concentrations in melancholia. Psychiatry Res 15:281–292, 1985

Rudduck C, Franzen G: Brief report: a new heritable fragile site on human chromosome 3. Hereditas 98:297–299, 1983

Rudduck C, Beckman L, Franzen G, et al: C3 and C6 complement types in schizophrenia. Hum Hered 35:255–258, 1985a

Rudduck C, Franzen G, Hanson A, et al: Gc serum groups in schizophrenia. Hum Hered 35:11–14, 1985b

Schulsinger F, Kety SS, Rosenthal D, et al: A family study of suicide, in Origin, Prevention, and Treatment of Affective Disorders. Edited by Shou M, Stromgren E. London, Academic Press, 1979, pp 277–287

Schulz B: Zur Erbpathologie der schizophrenie. Zeitschrift Gesammie Neurologie und Psychiatrie 143:175–293, 1932

Sedvall GC, Wode-Helgodt B: Aberrant monoamine metabolite levels in CSF and family history of schizophrenia. Arch Gen Psychiatry 37:1113–1116, 1980

Sedvall GC, Fyro B, Gullberg B, et al: Relationships in healthy volunteers between concentrations of monoamine metabolites in cerebrospinal fluid and family history of psychiatric morbidity. Br J Psychiatry 136:366–374, 1980

Sherington R, Brynjolfsson J, Petersson H, et al: Localization of a susceptibility locus for schizophrenia on chromosome 5. Nature 336:164–167, 1988

Singh TH, Rajkoma S: 49,XXXXY chromosome anomaly: an unusual variant of Klinefelter's syndrome. Br J Psychiatry 148:209–210, 1986

Sitaram N, Nurberger JI Jr, Gershon ES, et al: Faster cholinergic REM sleep induction in euthymic patients with primary affective illness. Science 208:200–202, 1980

Sitaram N, Jones D, Duke S, et al: Supersensitive ACTH REM-induction response as a genetic risk factor of depression. Paper presented at the annual meeting of the American College of Neuropsychopharmacology, San Juan, PR, December 10–14, 1984

Smeraldi E, Negri R, Heimbuch RC, et al: Familial patterns and possible modes of inheritance of primary affective disorders. J Affective Disord 3:173–182, 1981

Sperber MA: Schizophrenia and organic brain syndrome with trisomy 8 (group-C trisomy 8 [47,XX,8 +]). Biol Psychiatry 10:27–43, 1975

Sweeney D, Nelson C, Bowers M, et al: Delusional versus non-delusional depression: neurochemical differences. Lancet 2:100–101, 1978

Tanna VL, Winokur G, Elston RC, et al: A linkage study of depression spectrum disease: the use of the sib-pair method. Neuropsychobiology 2:52–62, 1976a

Tanna VL, Winokur G, Elston RC: A linkage study of pure depressive disease: the use of the sib-pair method. Biol Psychiatry 11:767–771, 1976b

Tanzi RE, Gusella FF, Watkins PC, et al: Amyloid beta-protein gene: cDNA, mRNA distribution, and genetic linkage near the Alzheimer locus. Science 235:880–884, 1987

Targum SD, Gershon ES, Van Eerdewegh M, et al: Human leukocyte antigen system not closely linked to or associated with bipolar manic-depressive illness. Biol Psychiatry 14:615–636, 1979

Targum SD, Rosen LN, DeLisi LE, et al: Cerebral ventricular size in major depressive disorder: association with delusional symptoms. Biol Psychiatry 18:329–336, 1983

Tienari P, Sorri A, Lahti I, et al: The Finnish adoptive family study of schizophrenia. Yale J Biol Med 58:227–237, 1985

Torgersen S: Genetic factors in moderately severe and mild affective disorder. Arch Gen Psychiatry 43:222–226, 1986

Traskman L, Asberg M, Bertilsson L, et al: Monoamine metabolites in CSF and suicidal behavior. Arch Gen Psychiatry 38:631–636, 1981

Tsuang MT: A study of pairs of sibs both hospitalized for mental disorder. Br J Psychiatry 113:283–300, 1967

Tsuang MT, Winokur G, Crowe RR: Morbidity risks of schizophrenia and affective disorders among first degree relatives of patients with schizophrenia, mania, depression, and surgical conditions. Br J Psychiatry 137:497–504, 1980

Tsuang MT, Farone SV, Fleming JA: Familial transmission of affective disorders: is there evidence supporting the dissociation between unipolar and bipolar disorders? Br J Psychiatry 146:268–271, 1985

Turner G, Gill R, Daniel A: Marker X chromosomes, mental retardation and macro-orchidism. N Engl J Med 299:1472, 1978

Turner WD: Genetic markers for schizotaxia. Biol Psychiatry 14:177–205, 1979

Van Kammen DP, Gelernter J: Biochemical instability in schizophrenia: I, the norepinephrine system, in Psychopharmacology: The Third Generation of Progress. Edited by Meltzer HY. New York, Raven Press, 1987, pp 745–751

Van Praag HM, de Hann S: Central serotonin metabolism and frequency of depression. Psychiatry Res 1:219–224, 1979

Von Knorring A-L, Cloninger CR, Bohman M, et al: An adoption study of depressive disorders and substance abuse. Arch Gen Psychiatry 40:943–950, 1983

Von Knorring L, Perris C, Oreland L, et al: Morbidity risks for psychiatric disorders in families of probands with affective disorders divided according to levels of platelet MAO activity. Psychiatry Res 15:271–279, 1985

Waters B, Thankar J, Lapierre Y: Erythrocyte lithium transport variables as a marker for manic-depressive disorder. Neuropsychobiology 9:94–98, 1983

Webb TP, Thake AI, Bundey SE, et al: A cytogenetic survey of a mentally retarded school age population with special reference to fragile sites. J Ment Defic Res 31 (part 1):61–71, 1987

Weinberger DR: Focal versus generalized pathology: results of quantitative MRI studies. Paper presented at the annual meeting of the American College of Neuropsychopharmacology, San Juan, December 1988

Weinshilbaum RM, Raymond FA: Inheritance of low erythrocyte catechol-O-methyltransferase activity in man. Am J Hum Genet 29:125–135, 1977

Weinshilbaum RM, Schrott HG, Raymond FA, et al: Inheritance of very low serum dopamine-beta-hydroxylase activity. Am J Hum Genet 27:573–585, 1975

Weissman MM, Gershon ES, Kiss KK, et al: Psychiatric disorders in the relaives of probands with affective disorders. Arch Gen Psychiatry 41:13–21, 1984

Weitkamp LR, Stancer HC, Persad E, et al: Depressive disorders and HLA: a gene on chromosome 6 that can affect behavior. N Engl J Med 305:1301–1306, 1981

White RL: DNA in medicine: human genetics. Lancet 2:1257–1262, 1984

Winokur G, Tanna VL: Possible role of X-linked dominant factor in manic-depressive illness. Diseases of the Nervous System 30:87–94, 1969

Wong DF, Wagner HN, Tune LE, et al: Positron emission tomography reveals elevated brain D-2 dopamine receptors in schizophrenia. Science 234:1558–1563, 1986

Woo SLC, Lidsky AS, Guttler F, et al: Cloned human phenylalanine hydroxylase gene allows prenatal diagnosis and carrier detection of classical phenylketonuria. Nature 306:151–155, 1983

Woo SLC, DiLella AG, Marvit J, et al: Molecular basis of phenylketonuria and potential somatic gene therapy. Cold Spring Harbor Symp Quant Biol 51:395–401, 1986

Wyatt RJ, Murphy DL, Belmaker R, et al: Reduced monoamine oxidase in platelets: a possible market for vulnerability to schizophrenia. Science 179:916–918, 1973

Zarcone VP, Benson KL, Berger PA: Abnormal rapid eye movement latencies in schizophrenia. Arch Gen Psychiatry 44:45–48, 1987

Zehnder M: Uber Krankheitsbild und Krankheitsverlauf bei schizophrenen Geschwistern. Monatschrift für Psychiatrie und Neurologie 103:231–277, 1941

Chapter 7

Pharmacological Treatment of Depression in Schizophrenia

Samuel G. Siris, M.D.

Chapter 7

Pharmacological Treatment of Depression in Schizophrenia

Schizophrenia is a devastating illness. Between 0.5% and 1% of the population have been reported to be affected (Blazer et al. 1985), usually beginning in late adolescence or early adulthood, and the disorder often runs a downhill course of social and vocational deterioration with enormous personal anguish as well as enormous economic burdens to be absorbed by families and communities.

Indeed, in so many cases, it is the social and vocational deterioration, and the anguish, that are the greatest tragedy of schizophrenia. Nonetheless, it has been the acute episodic manifestations of psychosis, such as hallucinations, delusions, and thought disorder, that have been the central focus of most of the research on schizophrenia during the past several decades. This is doubtless so, in large measure, because a relatively simple and efficacious treatment is available for many people with acute psychotic symptomatology: neuroleptic medications. Certainly neuroleptic medications have triggered a revolution in psychiatric care. Their containment of the most flagrant manifestations of psychosis has spawned an empirically validated basis for hope, a strategy for pathophysiologically based biomedical investigation, and a naively optimistic policy of deinstitutionalization.

Various descriptors have been used to refer to the state (or, more accurately, the states) of failure to thrive in the course of schizophrenia, including negative symptoms (Andreasen 1982; Andreasen and Olsen 1982; Lewine and Sommers 1985; Sommers 1985; Strauss et al. 1974), type II schizophrenia (Crow 1980), schizophrenia deficit state (Lewine and Sommers 1985; Sommers 1985), and postpsychotic depression (Knights and Hirsch 1981; McGlashan and Carpenter 1976; Roy et al. 1983; Siris et al. 1981). These conditions

This work was supported, in part, by grants MH-34309 and DA-05039.

represent a heterogeneous and overlapping set of conceptualizations for doubtless heterogeneous and overlapping sets of patients. The central common denominator of each of these categories, however, concerns how poorly these patients are doing in the social and vocational aspects of their lives, as well as how poorly they are doing in finding self-fulfillment and pleasure. This situation provides a monumental dilemma for clinicians, a source of suffering for patients, a heartache for families, a burden for the community, a hot potato for politicians, and a challenge for psychiatric researchers. This failure-to-thrive state, which is difficult to characterize and certainly difficult to treat, is now the "schizophrenia of schizophrenia."

Nevertheless, complex though it is, we need to have a systematic approach to treatment; this approach begins with a differential diagnosis. Assuming that potential medical etiologies for deterioration have been ruled out (and that is, of course, a crucial point), a number of psychiatric states remain to be considered in the differential diagnosis. These include 1) an organic cognitive and/or emotional deficit state, which is a component of these patients' biological diathesis; 2) an affective depression-like state, which is a component of the patients' diathesis (e.g., anhedonia has traditionally been considered to be a feature of schizophrenia, yet anhedonia is obviously an "affective" symptom); 3) a depression-like or negative symptom state, which is a neuroleptic side effect; 4) a transient disappointment reaction related to some real-life or intrapsychic event; 5) a syndrome of demoralization (Frank 1973), as might accompany other life-disrupting disorders; 6) depression-like or withdrawal behavior, which may be a component of a prodrome for the patient's next acute psychotic episode, and 7) a pattern of withdrawal, which represents an adaptation to chronic stress such as might result from continuing psychosis or possibly other stresses that might accompany schizophrenia.

This differential diagnosis is a difficult one. There are no well-validated clinical features that can unfailingly discriminate among all these possibilities. Yet each possibility would suggest a different treatment approach, and unfortunately some of these approaches might be mutually contradictory. There is no substitute for the clinician knowing the patient well, having a good working relationship with the patient, utilizing appropriate doses and durations of treatment, and being both open-minded and sensible in terms of evaluating the results that follow.

The topic of this chapter concerns pharmacotherapy. I will consequently forego a discussion of appropriate psychotherapy, family therapy, psychoeducation, and social or vocational rehabilitation approaches, which can often be invaluable in these patients. My pharmacological focus should not lead the reader to feel that these other approaches are unimportant, merely that the reader of this chapter is directed elsewhere to pursue them.

NEUROLEPTIC DOSAGE

The first psychopharmacological question involves neuroleptic choice and neuroleptic dosage. Low-potency and high-potency neuroleptics each have their problems in relationship to the topic at hand. Low-potency neuroleptics (i.e., chlorpromazine, thioridazine, mesoridazine) tend to be sedating. An oversedated patient may tend to sleep the day away, feel groggy, or have difficulty concentrating—any or all of which could contribute to a withdrawn, apathetic, demoralized, or even "depressed" picture. High-potency neuroleptics (i.e., essentially all other neuroleptics), on the other hand, have the problem of a higher incidence of extrapyramidal symptomatology. Patients suffering excessive stiffness may find it difficult to function socially as well as vocationally. Additional extrapyramidal symptomatology, in the form of akinesia and akathisia, may also occur. These are each so important in their own right that they will be discussed separately later in the chapter.

Determination of a patient's proper neuroleptic dosage is crucial. Too high a dose can result in zombie-like "negative symptoms" or depression-like states as a neuroleptic side effect. Too low a dose can allow the perpetuation of a psychosis with accompanying withdrawal, or allow for the progression of an incipient psychotic relapse. More usually, it is the first error that clinicians seem prone to make—giving more neuroleptic than is necessary—especially during ongoing maintenance phases of treatment. This fact was dramatically demonstrated in a study by Kane et al. (1983). In that study, patients felt to be appropriately maintained on fluphenazine decanoate were blindly randomized either to have that dose continued or to be switched to a one-tenth dilution. Remarkably, those patients who had their dose lowered went on to function better in social/vocational terms. Although by rating-scale criteria they suffered more relapses of psychosis, these relapses were rather gradual in onset and were easily contained by time-limited augmentation with additional oral neuroleptic. As a result, there were not more rehospitalizations in the low-dose group than in the standard-dose group. This general finding has also more recently been replicated by Marder et al. (1984) using a one-fifth dilution of fluphenazine decanoate. As a result, the first step to consider in a withdrawn, amotivational, or "depressed" schizophrenic patient who is not currently actively hallucinating or delusional is a lowering of the neuroleptic dosage. Improvement under these circumstances is unlikely to be immediate. More frequently, it will come gradually. This is especially the case if a depot neuroleptic has been employed, since the new steady state after a change of dose of depot neuroleptic may take from 3 to 6 months to be achieved (Marder et al. 1986).

Since change will come gradually, it is useful to have a reliable baseline impression of the schizophrenic patient before undertaking a change in medication. This will take at least two and possibly several visits spaced out in time. Such an approach will give both the clinician and the patient a much clearer and more meaningful impression of the true starting point and its range of variability—the changes inherent to which might otherwise be attributed to pharmacological issues if medication changes are abruptly undertaken. Such an approach will also aid in avoiding the pitfalls involved in two of the diagnoses included in our differential diagnosis list: transient disappointment reaction and *pre*psychotic depression or withdrawal. A transient disappointment reaction represents a more or less fleeting event that will resolve with the passage of time and, perhaps, a degree of nonspecific support and encouragement. Prepsychotic depression or withdrawal has been identified as a stage in the evolution of psychotic relapse (Docherty et al. 1978). It will declare itself soon enough if the patient is being closely followed and will, of course, usually call for an increase in neuroleptic medication as well as other appropriate interventions to forestall or ameliorate an episode of flagrant psychosis. Consequently, if a schizophrenic patient develops a fresh onset of withdrawn or "depressed" behavior, it is cause for following that patient with increased attention (e.g., more frequent visits) so that the meaning and course of that symptomatology can be evaluated.

EXTRAPYRAMIDAL SYNDROMES

Another issue related to neuroleptic medications is that they can lead to two extrapyramidal syndromes that can present as depression: akinesia and akathisia.

Akinesia

The term *akinesia* is somewhat confusing in that it has been used in two different ways in the literature. Originally, akinesia was defined in a more strictly motoric sense as being a neuroleptic-induced reduction in usual accessory motor movements (e.g., reduced arm swing, shuffling gait) (Chien et al. 1974). Later, Rifkin et al. (1975, 1978) and Van Putten and May (1978) used the term to refer to an extrapyramidally based loss of spontaneity not necessarily accompanied by any other extrapyramidal stigmata such as stiffness or cogwheeling. Such a syndrome can then present, not surprisingly, as a remarkable phenocopy for depression (Siris 1987). For example, a person with this form of akinesia may sit in front of a television set and not have enough spontaneity to turn it off or change the channel when the show he likes finishes and a less desirable program comes on. It is easy to see how such an individual begins to find life pleasureless and boring. Lack of spontaneity also interferes with a person's initiating conversations or comparable activities with other people. Again, life becomes empty, dull, and devoid of meaning. Such patients may feel that they have no one but themselves on which to blame these social failings. A person with this type of akinesia literally behaves "as if his starter motor is broken." In truth, such an individual does not make a very good friend, and others will fairly quickly drift away and abandon the person in favor of more interesting company. Moreover, motor manifestations of akinesia affect not simply the arms and legs. It is probably much more crucial and much more devastating socially that they can affect the muscles controlling facial expression. Facies, then, do not change, but tend to remain fixed in a more or less vacuous expression. Friends, family, and even clinicians may be misled into the assumption that "no one is home" emotionally when this occurs. This situation may be further compounded when the muscles concerned with vocal inflection are involved, leading the patient to speak in a dull, spacey monotone. Patients with this syndrome who do not know any better may soon start to agree with those who have abandoned them, thinking that they are not very good company and are not any fun to have around; they may, secondarily, stop trying because trying unsuccessfully is too painful. It is therefore imperative for the clinician to recognize akinesia when it occurs.

Indeed, it is particularly important to recognize akinesia because it may be simply treated. One way to treat akinesia, obviously, is by lowering the dose of neuroleptic medication. Another way to treat it is through the use of antiparkinsonian medication. In fact, the akinesia syndrome may respond virtually immediately to the institution of appropriate doses of antiparkinsonian medication—and in almost all cases respond within a few days to a week. This is thus one of the few psychiatric syndromes that will gratify both clinician and patient by responding with such rapidity.

Patients may even respond to a single im test dose of antiparkinsonian medication (e.g., 1 mg im of benztropine mesylate or equivalent). When given orally, doses of anticholinergic antiparkinsonian medication may be built up gradually, but must be built up to full therapeutic doses before they are deemed ineffective. Unfortunately, there is no definite dose that represents adequate treatment in all cases. This is the case largely because there is tremendous inter-individual variability in the metabolic breakdown of anticholinergic antiparkinsonian medication. Tune and Coyle (1980), for example, found a 10-fold variability in serum anticholinergic activity among subjects receiving benztropine 6 mg per day. Presumably the same effect would hold for other anticholinergic antiparkinsonian medi-cation. As a result, a sensible procedure is first to build a dosage up to 6 mg per day of benztropine or equivalent, unless, of course, the akinesia syndrome remits entirely at a lesser dose. This medication needs to be administered in divided doses (i.e., 2 mg po tid) inasmuch as the half-life is relatively brief (i.e., approximately 8 hours) so that adequate levels cannot otherwise be maintained over the diurnal period. If patients still do not respond to this dose, and if there are negligible anticholinergic side effects (i.e., blurry vision, dry mouth, constipation, or urinary hesitancy), this may be interpreted as pre-sumptive evidence that the patient is a rapid metabolizer, and the dose should be raised further. With caution, doses of 8, 10, or even 12 mg of benztropine per day may be attempted, with the clinician leveling off or reducing dosage if troublesome anticholinergic effects are observed. Obviously such an aggressive approach with anti-cholinergic antiparkinsonian drugs cannot be attempted if patients have specific contraindications (e.g., narrow angle glaucoma, pros-tatic hypertrophy, or cardiac conduction problems). But, in other cases, beneficial results can be remarkable. As a rough guide, the equivalencies of several of the commonly used anticholinergic anti-parkinsonian medications are given in Table 1 (Klett and Caffey

Table 1. Approximately Equivalent Doses of Commonly Available Anticholinergic Antiparkinsonian Medications

Generic	Brand	Dose (mg)
Benztropine	Cogentin	1
Trihexyphenidyl	Artane	2
Biperiden	Akineton	2
Procyclidine	Kemadrin	2
Ethopropazine	Parsidol	40
Diphenhydramine	Benadryl	50
Orphenadrine	Disipal	50

1972). These equivalencies are only approximate, however, and individual differences to which the clinician will need to be alert may
very well occur. The clinician must also be alert to the possibility of
noncompliance (either willful or unintentional) as a possible source
of lack of efficacy of antiparkinsonian medication. As a check against
this, pill-counts, a technique borrowed from clinical psychopharmacology research, can be a most effective measure and a powerful
nonverbal gesture to the patient about the importance of compliance.

Not infrequently, a patient's akinesia may respond to anticholinergic antiparkinsonian medication, but the patient is troubled by
one or more of the common anticholinergic side effects (Lake et al.
1986). Reduction in anticholinergic medication may provide the
answer, but if the antiakinesia effect is also then lost or reduced in
that patient, another approach may need to be taken. In such cases,
if the patient does not adapt to the anticholinergic side effects over
time (as often happens, resolving the problem), peripheral cholinomimetic agents may be of use. Bethanechol is such a systemic agent
that does not cross the blood-brain barrier. It may be useful in doses
ranging from 10 mg po bid to 25 mg po qid. Pilocarpine eye drops,
1%, 2 drops in each eye tid may be helpful for blurry vision. If this
does not provide relief, the concentration may be increased to 2%,
or then 4%. (Increasing the number of drops won't help because the
eye won't hold any more, even if they are put in, and the excess will
merely roll down the cheeks.) Interestingly, a drop or two of pilocarpine applied to the fingertip and then smeared on the gums tid
or qid will occasionally provide relief for the irritating symptom of
dry mouth. Alternatively, preparations of synthetic saliva are available
that may also provide relief of dry mouth when squirted into the
oral cavity qid, or even ad lib since these are physiological solutions.
Various laxatives, of course, may be useful for constipation, simple
Milk of Magnesia often being the most effective.

One additional bothersome side effect that anticholinergic antiparkinsonian agents may have, and that has only recently been at-
tended to, is reduction in memory—specifically reduction in free
recall memory (McEvoy et al. 1987; Perlick et al. 1986). Certainly
not all patients experience this effect, but for the ones who do it can
be disturbing. Since it is a central effect, of course, peripherally acting
cholinomimetic agents are not of use. If the antiakinesia effect is
substantial, the patient may still find some loss in memory to be
worth the bargain. Nevertheless, in such cases, some trial and error
by the clinician and the patient will be indicated to find the optimal
agent and/or dosage. One reassuring factor is that even if memory
effects occur with anticholinergic medications, they are not perma-

nent but will last only as long as the anticholinergic medication continues to be administered.

One alternative to anticholinergic antiparkinsonian medication is amantadine. Amantadine is a dopamine agonist thought to affect nigrostriatal dopamine synapses specifically, sparing mesolimbic dopamine synapses, and thus able to reverse neuroleptic parkinsonian side effects without aggravating the psychosis (Bailey and Stone 1975). However, unfortunately, it is possible that amantadine may in fact re-exacerbate psychotic symptomatology in a small number of cases (Nestelbaum et al. 1986). Nevertheless, it is likely that amantadine may be useful in treating at least some cases of akinesia, although this specific use of amantadine has never been tested prospectively in a properly controlled double-blind trial.

Treatment of akinesia is a long-term issue in neuroleptic therapy. As opposed to other extrapyramidal side effects that are usually more acute in onset and dramatic in presentation, akinesia may be subtle in its manifestations and insidious in onset. Notably, as mentioned above, it sometimes may occur in the absence of stiffness, cogwheeling, or other motoric extrapyramidal phenomena. Since akinesia may present as a clinical phenocopy of depression or negative symptoms in schizophrenic patients, a thorough course of antiparkinsonian treatment should be carried out in any such patients as a therapeutic trial. Long-term antiparkinsonian treatment then may be necessary in patients who require maintenance neuroleptics to circumvent the social and vocational ravages of akinesia. There is a somewhat inconclusive literature concerning the abuse potential of anticholinergic antiparkinsonian medications (McEvoy 1983). (i.e., Do patients sometimes take more medication than prescribed because it makes them feel better than they should, or merely because it reduces akinesia and makes them feel more normal, which they naturally prefer?) Nevertheless, maintenance antiparkinsonian medication is indicated in this circumstance if it ameliorates akinesia. The side effects of antiparkinsonian medications are acute, not cumulative, and will resolve whenever the medication is stopped. Anticholinergic medications will, to be sure, lower the threshold for expression of tardive dyskinesia, as would be expected on the basis of the relevant cholinergic/dopaminergic balance in the basal ganglia; but anticholinergic medications do not contribute causally to tardive dyskinesia. Therefore, if anything, anticholinergic medications constitute an "early warning" challenge for tardive dyskinesia—letting patients with a proneness to tardive dyskinesia manifest aspects of the symptomatology earlier than they might if treated with neuroleptic alone, at a stage when it will disappear with withdrawal of the anticholinergic medication, but alerting the clinician and patient to the possibility of an incipient problem in this regard.

Akathisia

A second extrapyramidal side effect of neuroleptic medications that can present at times subtly (Siris 1985) and at times with notable dysphoric symptomatology (Van Putten and Marder 1987; Van Putten et al. 1984) is akathisia. Classically, akathisia is a syndrome of uncomfortable motor restlessness, often felt more in the legs than in other muscle groups. In its full-blown expression it is hard to miss, as a patient may pace a great deal and find it difficult to sit still for an interview or for other activities, or merely find it terribly difficult to relax. But even then, it can sometimes be quite problematic to distinguish akathisia from severe anxiety or psychotic agitation. Usually, though, with careful questioning, the patient is able to appreciate the distinctly physical character of the restlessness in florid akathisia. As the opposite side of the akinesia coin, perhaps, a patient with akathisia has "a starter motor that won't stop." This is a side effect that can be quite subjectively disturbing as well as socially incapacitating, and cases of suicide have been documented to have been associated with akathisia (Drake and Ehrlich 1985; Shear et al. 1983). It is not well-known how protean the subtler manifestations of akathisia might be, but it is certainly a consideration to be included on any list of the differential diagnosis of dysphoric or dysfunctional states among schizophrenic patients being maintained on neuroleptic medications.

As is the case with akinesia, the preferred treatment for akathisia is the reduction of neuroleptic dose, as long as this can be accomplished without re-exacerbation of psychotic symptomatology. Akathisia may also respond to anticholinergic antiparkinsonian medication or amantadine, and vigorous treatment with these agents can be pursued, but unfortunately the response rate is less than is the case with akinesia and other extrapyramidal side effects. However, there are some other psychopharmacological interventions that can also be attempted to deal with akathisia. Not infrequently, akathisia may respond to the addition of propranolol (Adler et al. 1986; Comaty 1987; Dupuis et al. 1987; Lipinsky et al. 1984). To treat akathisia, a starting dose of 20 mg per day may be tried in divided doses, with doses increasing by 10 to 20 mg per day every few days until symptoms ameliorate or side effects supervene. Responses are usually observed at doses of 80 mg per day or less. At these relatively low doses, the usual problematic side effect of propranolol, orthostatic hypotension, is usually not seen. Nevertheless, it is still prudent to monitor the patient's pulse and blood pressure lying or sitting and standing with each change in dose. Doses should not be raised if the pulse is less than 50 or the systolic blood pressure is less than 90. Other beta blockers have also been reported to be useful in akathisia (Dupuis et al. 1987; Ratey et al. 1985), but it is doubtful if any are superior to propranolol. One potential problem with the use of propranolol or other beta blockers is that they might predispose to depression-like symptoms as a side effect of their own, and the clinician should be alert for this if it occurs.

Finally, benzodiazepines may possibly at times be useful in treating akathisia (Gagrat et al. 1978), and an empirical approach may be followed with any of several drugs from this class. Whatever pharmacological agents are employed, a vigorous approach to the treatment of akathisia is indicated because considerable functional impairment as well as subjective suffering may result from unrecognized or untreated cases.

ANTIDEPRESSANT MEDICATIONS

Not all manifestations of depression-like symptomatology in schizophrenia occur on an extrapyramidal basis, of course, at least insofar as we can establish the origin in terms of medication response. The logical question that follows, then, is whether any of this depression-like symptomatology is responsive to traditional antidepressant medications. For the purposes of this chapter, I will restrict my discussion to depression-like symptomatology that occurs subsequent to the resolution or partial resolution of flagrant psychotic episodes. (Depression-like symptomatology may also occur prominently during the height of flagrant psychosis, and its treatment at those times is a topic unto itself that challenges our capacity sensibly to determine how, or even whether, to draw boundaries among such categories as: schizophrenia with features of dysphoria; schizophrenia with emotional turmoil, including aspects of depression; schizoaffective disorder, mainly schizophrenic; schizoaffective disorder, mainly affective; and psychotic depression.)

The appropriate use of antidepressants in schizophrenia is a topic that has been understudied in the age of psychopharmacology. At least in part, this is due to biases that operate against consideration of such treatment. The first bias is that, since the formulations of Kraepelin, the bedrock of psychiatric nosology has been the distinction between manic-depressive illness (i.e., depression in this case) and dementia praecox, now known as schizophrenia. Thus the notion that antidepressants may have a role in the treatment of an aspect of schizophrenia, or even in the treatment of a complication in the course of schizophrenia for certain individuals, would seem to offend an axiom of our science. Of course, that is not really the case. One important reason why it is not really the case has to do with the second bias, which has limited the scope of investigating the use of antidepressants in schizophrenia. That bias is that antidepressants are specifically linked to depression per se. That patently is not true. Depression is not some form of "imipramine deficiency syndrome." Nevertheless, this oversimplified bias of thinking delayed recognition of the usefulness of antidepressants in the psychiatric syndrome of panic anxiety since patients with panic disorder were not necessarily "depressed." We must realize that if imipramine had first been found to be useful in panic disorder, tricyclics as a class might have come to be referred to as antipanic medications, and we might only now be discovering their efficacy in depression. Thus it need not offend our diagnostic sensibilities for a medication to be useful in more than one condition. (For that matter, the molecular structure of tricyclic antidepressants, of course, is remarkably close to that of neuroleptic medications, and all the various activities of these psychoactive molecules have doubtless not as yet been elucidated.) In essence, then, the real issue for clinical care rests on the empirical validation of the therapeutic efficacy of the compounds we employ.

The broad general topic of the use of antidepressants in schizophrenia has been reviewed (Siris et al. 1978), but few studies have focused prospectively on the treatment of depression-like symptoms per se in a double-blind design, among patients concomitantly being maintained on neuroleptics. Published studies that meet these criteria are outlined in Table 2. Unfortunately, most of these studies did not make an organized attempt to eliminate the confounding of akinesia with a standardized trial of antiparkinsonian medication. Most of these studies also did not measure plasma levels of antidepressant medications in an attempt to document the adequacy of the treatment trial.

As seen in Table 2, three of the six studies were generally positive and three generally negative. The negative study of maprotiline (Waehrens and Gerlach 1980) can be questioned on the basis of the possible inadequacy of the maprotiline dose (i.e., doses as low as 50 mg per day). On the other hand, the negative nortriptyline study (Johnson 1981) can be questioned on the basis of how high the dose of nortriptyline was (i.e., 150 mg per day). That dose of nortriptyline would be likely to result in a number of patients having plasma levels in excess of the putative "therapeutic window" of 50 to 150 ng/ml, which has been described in patients with primary nondelusional unipolar depressions (American Psychiatric Association Task Force

Table 2. Double-Blind Studies of Antidepressants in "Depressed" Schizophrenic Patients

Reference	N	Patients	Neuroleptic	Antidepressant	Duration	Result
Singh et al. (1978)	60	Feighner criteria for schizophrenia Chronic patients with symptoms of depression HDRS score of 18 or more	Continuation of previous phenothiazine	Trazodone 300 mg/day or placebo	6 weeks	HDRS and CGI changes favored trazodone No significant differences in BPRS
Prusoff et al., (1979)	35	New Haven Index Schizophrenia A score of at least 7 on the Raskin Depression Rating Scale	Perphenazine 16–48 mg/day	Amitriptyline 100–200 mg/day or placebo	1,2,4, or 6 months	Some decrease in depression ratings Some increase in thought disorder and agitation ratings Overall impression: mildly positive
Waehrens and Gerlach (1980)	17	No diagnostic criteria given Patients were chronic and "emotionally withdrawn"	Continuation of previous neuroleptic	Maprotiline 50–200 mg/day or placebo (cross-over design)	8 weeks	No benefit to adding maprotiline

Table 2. Double-Blind Studies of Antidepressants in "Depressed" Schizophrenic Patients (continued)

Reference	N	Patients	Neuroleptic	Antidepressant	Duration	Result
Johnson (1981)	50	Feighner or Schneiderian symptoms of schizophrenia All chronic patients Beck Depression Inventory score of 15 or more	Fluphenazine decanoate or flupenthixol decanoate	Nortriptyline 150 mg/day or placebo	5 weeks	No alleviation of depression with nortriptyline Increased side effects with nortriptyline
Becker (1983)	52	RDC for schizophrenia RDC for major depressive syndrome (superimposed on schizophrenia)	Chlorpromazine 100–1,200 mg/day or thiothixene 5–60 mg/day	Imipramine 150–250 mg/day for patients on chlorpromazine or placebo for patients on thiothixene	4 weeks (after 2 weeks drug free)	Both treatments effective compared to baseline on BPRS and HDRS Neither treatment statistically superior to the other on BPRS or HDRS More sedative and autonomic side effects in chlorpromazine/imipramine group

Table 2. Double-Blind Studies of Antidepressants in "Depressed" Schizophrenic Patients (continued)

Reference	N	Patients	Neuroleptic	Antidepressant	Duration	Result
Siris et al. (1987a)	33	RDC for schizophrenia or schizoaffective disorder RDC for major or minor depression (while patient is nonpsychotic or residually psychotic) Does not respond to benztropine 2 mg po tid	Fluphenazine decanoate, clinically adjusted weekly dose	Imipramine 150–200 mg/day or placebo	6 weeks	Imipramine group statistically superior to placebo on CGI and each of four depression subscales No difference between groups on measures of psychosis or side effects No relationship apparent between tricyclic plasma levels and clinical response

Note. HDRS = Hamilton Depression Rating Scale; CGI = Clinical Global Impression; BPRS = Brief Psychiatric Rating Scale; RDC = Research Diagnostic Criteria.

1985). This is even more likely to be the case since neuroleptic medications are known to raise tricyclic antidepressant plasma levels on the basis of competing for their hepatic metabolic pathways (Kragh-Sorenson et al. 1977; Siris et al. 1982). Of course it also needs to be recognized that a therapeutic range or threshold has only been suggested for certain tricyclics and only in the case of primary non-delusional unipolar depressions. Ranges or thresholds in other types of depression, such as secondary depressions or depressions in patients who also manifest psychotic symptomatology, or in patients also receiving neuroleptic medications, have never been identified (Siris et al. 1988a). The final negative study included in Table 2 (Becker 1983) utilized a different neuroleptic for those patients who received an antidepressant than for those patients who did not. Because of this, the results of that study are difficult to interpret, especially since a rather strongly anticholinergic neuroleptic, chlor-promazine, was combined with a strongly anticholinergic antidepressant, amitriptyline, and then compared with a relatively non-anticholinergic neuroleptic, thiothixene.

On the other side of the coin, the studies suggesting a utility for supplemental tricyclic antidepressants in cases of postpsychotic depression, while positive, are not overwhelmingly so. Even the most encouraging of these three studies showed only half of the anti-depressant-treated patients to be substantially improved (versus an approximately 10% placebo response rate) (Siris et al. 1987a). It is not clear why only half of the patients respond, or what the selective characteristics are of those patients who do respond (Siris et al. 1987b). Nevertheless, it is encouraging that at least some of the patients benefit from such a trial—and it is clearly a clinically valuable trial for those who do respond. Encouraging also is the fact that these studies have not found exacerbation of psychosis by adjunctive tricyclic antidepressants to be a limiting drawback (Siris et al. 1987a). It is further noteworthy that the only one of the studies in Table 2 that made an organized attempt to eliminate akinesia as a confounding factor was the study that most strongly showed an advantageous effect to the addition of a supplemental antidepressant (Siris et al. 1987a). It is possible that a tricyclic antidepressant may show the most benefit when used in patients who are receiving an appropriate concomitant antiparkinsonian medication with their neuroleptic (Siris et al. 1983).

In a smaller number of studies, monoamine oxidase (MAO) inhibitors have been tried in the treatment of schizophrenia (Brenner and Shopsin 1980; Siris et al. 1978). Most of these studies have suffered from a number of methodological problems, which may make their interpretation difficult. The main problem is that, for our purposes, none of these studies was particularly oriented around investigating the effects of an MAO inhibitor on specifically depression-like syndromes in well-diagnosed schizophrenic patients. While no controlled MAO inhibitor study has been especially promising in schizophrenia, it is also noteworthy that these studies have not reported exacerbations of psychoses.

A preliminary conclusion for the existing literature would be the following: A trial of an antidepressant should be considered for a patient with schizophrenia when a nonpsychotic, or only residually psychotic, patient manifests a syndrome that, with the exception of schizophrenic features, is a phenocopy of depression in a nonschizophrenic patient. Judging that phenocopy requires clinical skill, of course, because these patients may be difficult to get to know and may be somewhat idiosyncratic in the way they express themselves. Nevertheless, a proper clinical interview in these patients can readily elicit such symptoms as dysphoric mood, low energy level, poor pleasure capacity, sleep or appetite changes, feelings of guilt, and low self-esteem. Patients should first be stabilized on an appropriate dose of neuroleptic, receive a full trial of antiparkinsonian medication, and be followed for several weeks before the initiation of an antidepressant trial. If the syndrome of depression persists, an antidepressant may be added. It is probably best to build up the antidepressant dose gradually, but it should be built up to the full antidepressant dose, and maintained for an adequate trial duration. Patients should be observed carefully during such a treatment trial. If mild psychotic symptoms emerge, it does not necessarily mean that the antidepressant must be discontinued. Often such mild exacerbations can be managed successfully by making a small increment in the neuroleptic dosage, while preserving other beneficial antidepressant effects. Not all patients will respond, of course, but for those who do the results can be quite significant clinically. It has not been established by properly controlled comparisons which antidepressant is the most useful in this situation—if, indeed, there are any meaningful differences among the various antidepressant agents. The most positive of the controlled double-blind reports, however, involved imipramine. In terms of the best neuroleptic to use during a trial of such combined treatment, a high-potency neuroleptic would be advisable in most cases to try to avoid the accumulation of excessive anticholinergic activity that could potentially result when combining a neuroleptic, an antidepressant, and an antiparkinsonian medication.

SELF-MEDICATION

A discussion of the pharmacological treatments of depression in schizophrenia would not be complete without including those agents that patients administer to themselves. One of the most common of these substances is coffee. A number of patients make a habit of consuming 10, 12, or even more cups of coffee per day, and in such cases the self-administration of caffeine is really quite considerable. If these cases represent overmedication with neuroleptics, unrecognized akinesia, or secondary depression in schizophrenia, they are probably best dealt with in the ways described above, appropriate to those conditions. In other cases we ought to wonder if these patients may know something we don't in terms of their own pharmacological management. Especially for those patients who find it very hard to "get going" in the morning, as so many patients on neuroleptics in fact do, a cup or two of coffee first thing on waking can provide a much needed boost.

It is common knowledge that the other substance schizophrenic patients use heavily is tobacco. It is possible that these patients are trying to do with nicotine something similar to what they themselves, or other patients, are trying to do with coffee. A problem here, of course, is that cigarette smoking is intrinsically harmful and should be discouraged on medical grounds. It is also possible that many of these patients, by their smoking, may be inducing enzymes to more rapidly metabolize their neuroleptic drugs, with which they are being iatrogenically overdosed. If that is the case, the obviously better answer is for neuroleptic doses to be directly lowered.

It is interesting that schizophrenic patients also seem to have a propensity for selecting stimulant rather than sedative substances of abuse when they turn to illicit "street psychopharmacology" (Schneier and Siris 1987; Siris et al. 1988b). In a way, this seems counterintuitive. Stimulant substances such as amphetamines or cocaine would be expected to exacerbate psychosis, and schizophrenic patients experience psychosis as terrifying and decidedly unpleasant. The fact, therefore, that they would deliberately select stimulant substances to abuse, risking the exacerbation of their psychosis, suggests that seeking pharmacological relief of some other unpleasant condition, be it dysphoria or anhedonia or lethargy, must be rather compelling and that stimulant substances must have some at least transient effect on this. Clearly much remains to be learned about relevance of stimulants to the dysphoric states that can arise either in schizophrenia or in response to the neuroleptic medications with which schizophrenia is treated.

In summary, the treatment of depression in schizophrenia has emerged in recent years as an important clinical question, as it has been recognized to what extent depression-like symptomatology can lead to morbidity, impaired functioning, or even mortality in those patients. Modern operationalized diagnostic criteria have allowed this condition to be described so that it can be studied, and differential pharmacoresponsivity has provided a strategy whereby several of the various conditions presenting with this syndrome can be distinguished and rational psychopharmacological treatment plans developed.

REFERENCES

Adler L. Angrist B, Peselow E, et al: A controlled assessment of propranolol in the treatment of neuroleptic-induced akathisia. Br J Psychiatry 149:42–45, 1986

American Psychiatric Association Task Force on the Use of Laboratory Tests in Psychiatry: Tricyclic antidepressants: blood level measurements and clinical outcome: an APA task force report. Am J Psychiatry 142:155–162, 1985

Andreasen NC: Negative symptoms in schizophrenia: definition and reliability. Arch Gen Psychiatry 39:784–788, 1982

Andreasen NC, Olsen S: Negative vs positive schizophrenia: definition and validation. Arch Gen Psychiatry 39:789–794, 1982

Bailey EV, Stone JW: The mechanism of action of amantadine in parkinsonism: a review. Arch Int Pharmacodyn Ther 216:246–262, 1975

Becker RE: Implications of the efficacy of thiothixene and a chlorpromazine-imipramine combination for depression in schizophrenia. Am J Psychiatry 140:208–211, 1983

Blazer D, George LK, Landerman R, et al: Psychiatric disorders: a rural/urban comparison. Arch Gen Psychiatry 42:651–656, 1985

Brenner R, Shopsin B: The use of monoamine oxidase inhibitors in schizophrenia. Biol Psychiatry 15:633–647, 1980

Chien CP, DiMascio A, Cole JO: Antiparkinson agents and depot phenothiazines. Am J Psychiatry 131:86–90, 1974

Comaty JE: Propranolol treatment of neuroleptic-induced akathisia. Psychiatric Annals 17:150–153, 1987

Crow TJ: Molecular pathology of schizophrenia: more than one disease process? Br Med J [Clin Res] 280:66–68, 1980

Docherty JP, van Kammen DP, Siris SG, et al: Stages of onset of acute schizophrenic psychosis. Am J Psychiatry 135:720–726, 1978

Drake RE, Ehrlich J: Suicide attempts associated with akathisia. Am J Psychiatry 142:499–501, 1985

Dupuis B, Catteau J, Dumon J-P, et al: Comparison of propranolol, sotalol, and betaxolol in the treatment of neuroleptic-induced akathisia. Am J Psychiatry 144:802–805, 1987

Frank JD: Persuasion and Healing. Baltimore, Johns Hopkins University Press, 1973

Gagrat D, Hamilton J, Belmaker RH: Intravenous diazepam in the treatment of neuroleptic-induced acute dystonia and akathisia. Am J Psychiatry 135:1232–1233, 1978

Johnson DAW: Studies of depressive symptoms in schizophrenia. Br J Psychiatry 139:89–101, 1981

Kane JM, Rifkin A, Woerner M, et al: Low-dose neuroleptic treatment of outpatient schizophrenics: I, preliminary results for relapse rates. Arch Gen Psychiatry 40:893–896, 1983

Klett CJ, Caffey E Jr: Evaluating the long-term need for antiparkinson drugs by chronic schizophrenics. Arch Gen Psychiatry 26:374–379, 1972

Knights A, Hirsch SR: "Revealed" depression and drug treatment for schizophrenia. Arch Gen Psychiatry 38:806–811, 1981

Kragh-Sorenson P, Borga G, Carle L, et al: Effect of simultaneous treatment with low doses of perphenazine on plasma and urine concentrations of nortriptyline and 10-hydroxynortriptyline. Eur J Clin Pharmacol 11:479–483, 1977

Lake CR, Casey DE, McEvoy JP, et al: Anticholinergic prophylaxis in young adults treated with neuroleptic drugs. Psychopharmacol Bull 22:981–984, 1986

Lewine RRJ, Sommers AA: Clinical definition of negative symptoms as a reflection of theory and methodology, in Controversies in Schizophrenia: Changes and Consistencies. Edited by Alpert M. New York, Guilford Press, 1985, pp 267–276

Lipinsky JF, Zubenko GS, Cohen BM, et al: Propranolol in the treatment of neuroleptic-induced akathisia. Am J Psychiatry 141:412–415, 1984

Marder SR, Van Putten T, Mintz J, et al: Costs and benefits of two doses of fluphenazine. Arch Gen Psychiatry 41:1025–1029, 1984

Marder SR, Hawes EM, Van Putten T, et al: Fluphenazine plasma levels in patients receiving low and conventional doses of fluphenazine decanoate. Psychopharmacology 88:480–483, 1986

McEvoy JP: The clinical use of anticholinergic drugs as treatment for extrapyramidal side effects of neuroleptic drugs. J Clin Pharmacol 3:288–302, 1983

McEvoy JP, McCue M, Spring B, et al: Effects of amantadine and trihexyphenidyl on memory in elderly normal volunteers. Am J Psychiatry 144:573–577, 1987

McGlashan TH, Carpenter WT Jr: Post-psychotic depression in schizophrenia. Arch Gen Psychiatry 33:231–241, 1976

Nestelbaum Z, Siris SG, Rifkin A, et al: Exacerbation of schizophrenia associated with amantadine. Am J Psychiatry 143:1170–1171, 1986

Perlick D, Stastny P, Katz I, et al: Memory deficits and anticholinergic levels in chronic schizophrenia. Am J Psychiatry 143:230–232, 1986

Prusoff BA, Williams DH, Weissman MM, et al: Treatment of secondary depression in schizophrenia. Arch Gen Psychiatry 36:569–575, 1979

Ratey JJ, Sorgi P, Polakoff S: Nadolol as a treatment for akathisia. Am J Psychiatry 142:640–642, 1985

Rifkin A, Quitkin F, Klein DF: Akinesia: a poorly recognized drug-induced extrapyramidal behavioral disorder. Arch Gen Psychiatry 32:672–674, 1975

Rifkin A, Quitkin F, Kane J, et al: Are prophylactic antiparkinson drugs necessary? A controlled study of procyclidine withdrawal. Arch Gen Psychiatry 35:483–489, 1978

Roy A, Thompson R, Kennedy S: Depression in chronic schizophrenia. Br J Psychiatry 142:465–470, 1983

Schneier FR, Siris SG: A review of psychoactive substance use and abuse in schizophrenia: patterns of drug choice. J Nerv Ment Dis 175:641–652, 1987

Shear MK, Frances A, Weiden P: Suicide associated with akathisia and depot fluphenazine treatment. J Clin Psychopharmacol 3:235–236, 1983

Singh AN, Saxena B, Nelson HL: A controlled clinical study of trazodone in chronic schizophrenic patients with pronounced depressive symptomatology. Current Therapy Research 23:485–501, 1978

Siris SG: Akathisia and "acting-out." J Clin Psychiatry 46:395–397, 1985

Siris SG: Akinesia and post-psychotic depression: a difficult differential diagnosis. J Clin Psychiatry 48:240–243, 1987

Siris SG, van Kammen DP, Docherty JP: Use of antidepressant drugs in schizophrenia. Arch Gen Psychiatry 35:1368–1377, 1978

Siris SG, Harmon GK, Endicott J: Post-psychotic depressive symptoms in hospitalized schizophrenic patients. Arch Gen Psychiatry 38:1122–1123, 1981

Siris SG, Cooper TB, Rifkin AE, et al: Plasma imipramine concentrations in patients receiving concomitant fluphenazine decanoate. Am J Psychiatry 139:104–106, 1982

Siris SG, Rifkin A, Reardon GT, et al: Comparative side effects to imipramine, benztropine, or their combination, in patients receiving fluphenazine decanoate. Am J Psychiatry 140:1069–1071, 1983

Siris SG, Morgan V, Fagerstrom R, et al: Adjunctive imipramine in the treatment of post-psychotic depression: a controlled trial. Arch Gen Psychiatry 44:533–539, 1987a

Siris SG, Adan F, Cohen M, et al: Targeted treatment of depression-like symptoms in schizophrenia. Psychopharmacol Bull 23:85–89, 1987b

Siris SG, Sellew AP, Frechen K, et al: Antidepressants in the treatment of post-psychotic depression in schizophrenia: drug interactions and other considerations. Journal of Clinical Chemistry 34:837–840, 1988a

Siris SG, Kane JM, Frechen K, et al: Histories of substance abuse in patients with post-psychotic depressions. Compr Psychiatry 29:550–557, 1988b

Sommers AA: Negative symptoms: conceptual and methodological problems. Schizophr Bull 11:364–377, 1985

Strauss J, Carpenter WT Jr, Bartko J: The diagnosis and understanding of schizophrenia: part III, speculations on the processes that underlie schizophrenic symptoms and signs. Schizophr Bull 1:61–69, 1974

Tune L, Coyle JT: Serum levels of anticholinergic drugs in the treatment of acute extrapyramidal side effects. Arch Gen Psychiatry 37:293–297, 1980

Van Putten T, Marder SR: Behavioral toxicity of antipsychotic drugs. J Clin Psychiatry 48:9 (suppl):13–19, 1987

Van Putten T, May PR: "Akinetic depression" in schizophrenia. Arch Gen Psychiatry 35:1101–1107, 1978

Van Putten T, May PRA, Marder SR: Akathisia with haloperidol and thiothixene. Arch Gen Psychiatry 41:1036–1039, 1984

Waehrens J, Gerlach J: Antidepressant drugs in anergic schizophrenia: a double-blind cross-over study with maprotiline and placebo. Acta Psychiatr Scand 61:438–444, 1980

DATE DUE